"I enjoyed Fr. Morwood's attempt to 'push the envelope' on the fundamental ways that we approach the images and articulation of our Catholic doctrine, and our understanding of that doctrine in our daily lives. I particularly appreciated his courage and forthrightness in criticizing some aspects of the Catholic Catechism, particularly its use of outdated imagery and language from a worldview that is no longer relevant or applicable to our present situation. *Tomorrow's Catholic* will help generate some important discussion and reflection on future imaging and ways of articulating our shared faith."

Rev. John Heagle
Co-Director, TARA Center

"Michael Morwood's book is a must reading for today's Catholics. He addresses the major issues facing Christians who must live in a world of many religions: what say you Jesus of Nazareth? He brings that technical theological discussion down to the level of the everyday Catholic, writing in clear and easily understandable pastoral style. Those who read Morwood's book will be forever changed and, like myself, truly in his debt."

Dick Westley
author of *Redemptive Intimacy: A New Perspective for the Journey to Adult Faith* and *Morality and Its Beyond*

"Father Morwood's attentiveness to our struggles and continuing search for God has been cultivated by extensive pastoral ministry both at home in Australia and in North America. For him the world is not a peril for Christian faith, nor is the Church just a sinful community in need of conversion. He invites us with disarming directness to draw upon our day-to-day experiences of life to discover the present yet hidden God communicated through Jesus."

Michael A. Fahey, S.J.
Professor of Theology
Marquette University

D1023882

TOMORROW'S CATHOLIC

Understanding God and Jesus in a New Millennium

MICHAEL MORWOOD, MSC

TWENTY-THIRD PUBLICATIONS
BAYARD Mystic, CT 06355

Fifth printing 2001

Twenty-Third Publications
A Division of Bayard
185 Willow Street
P.O. Box 180
Mystic, CT 06355
(860) 536-2611
(800) 321-0411

ISBN 0-89622-724-3
Library of Congress Catalog Card Number 97-60027
Printed in the U.S.A.

Foreword

Every generation of humankind thinks of its own age as momentous, and why not? This is "our" time and our only one. Perceiving our era as a milestone in history is part of insisting on our own significance. Yet, at least with hindsight, it does seem that there are major turning points in the human story, times when profound shifts occur and things are never the same again. All the social commentators assure us that ours is such an era.

The coming of a new millennium is a milestone in its own right, but regardless of the date on the Western calendar there is ample warrant to propose that a new age is emerging in human consciousness and living. One can recite a long list of the signs of a paradigm shift—as the social scientists call it—but I cite just one to symbolize the rest: the World Wide Web. What a revolution this represents in human communications; truly the global village has arrived.

Michael Morwood's book *Tomorrow's Catholic* is a courageous attempt to interface the ancient and rich tradition of Catholic faith "with the great social and scientific developments of our age." He is convinced, and rightly so, that "the package" of Catholicism we received from the previous era is no longer adequate to the challenges of this age. Epitomized in "blind obedience to church authority," much of it simply won't "work" for our time.

To refashion Catholicism to meet the challenges of this new era requires imagination and courage, and Morwood demonstrates both.

Jesus counseled that "every scribe who has been trained for the reign of God" must be ever ready "to draw from the storeroom of both the old and the new" (Matthew 13:52). Morwood dips into the rich treasury of Catholic faith to find the "old and new" that can rise to the occasion for our time.

Oh, but it will surely require us to embrace the Paschal Mystery in our personal lives and as a faith community. We will have to die to many old ways and thought patterns if we are to rise up as "tomorrow's Catholics." If we cling to the old ways too tenaciously, if we confuse earthen vessels for the treasures they hold, we may be in mortal danger of losing everything. On the other hand, if we are willing to let go of what is no longer adequate, to cherish what is constitutive but to hold the rest loosely, then, as the gospel promises, we will find new life.

Though I don't remember him saying it anywhere, Michael Morwood's book is an elaboration of a "radical" theology of baptism; it calls us to the personal and communal conversion required to become a church of responsible, adult Catholic Christians, participating fully in Jesus' mission today and working for God's reign in the present world. Baptism as a call to such personal and social transformation, of course, is an ancient theology, going back to the very beginning of the church and is now, again, its official teaching (see the *Catechism of the Catholic Church* for a "radical" understanding of baptism). But we are still far from realizing such a theology in the institutional church itself or in the spirituality of our people.

Written in very readable language and with a conversational style, *Tomorrow's Catholic* invites us to take some bold steps in the right direction—to honor what our baptism and this ancient faith might mean in a world of www.com.

Thomas H. Groome
Professor of Theology and Religious Education,
Boston College

CONTENTS

Tomorrow's Catholic

Introduction

We are living through what may well be the greatest time of change in Christian history. In the Catholic Church there has been an extraordinary breakdown of the religious culture which shaped Catholic identity for many adults. There is unprecedented division of opinion among us, as well as unprecedented disagreement with and questioning of church authority on matters concerning faith and morals. At the same time, we are conscious of the spirit of Pentecost moving among us, and we are aware of the challenge to be the church in a new millennium. It is an exciting time, yet it is also a time of tension. It is a time when inevitably many will look back and long for the security of the past. It is a time of uncertainty, but also a time of great potential.

The upheaval and change we have experienced and will continue to experience as Catholics are not simply the result of movements or events within the church. External influences have contributed to the present situation in no small way, and it is vitally important to recognize this. Failure to do so can cause people to look for easy solutions to the tensions and disagreements created by the breakdown of previously uniform Catholic practice. It can lead to blaming particular groups within the church for the church's present problems. It can cause some Catholics to put their hopes in a "restorationist" policy to solve the problems, i.e., wanting to move back to the days of strong order and authority, of unquestioning obedience, and more visible signs of Catholic identity, such as the return to confession or forms of devotional practice. It can blind us to the urgent need to come to terms with the great social and scientific developments of our age. The reality is that if the Christian message is to be relevant to people educated within a social and scientific worldview simply unimaginable in the early part of the twentieth century, it is essential to have some understanding of these developments and integrate them with the basics of the Christian message.

Much of the Catholic "package" of beliefs, attitudes, and practices we inherited in our Catholic upbringing was shaped at a time when the church was at the center of western society and when its authority was unquestioned. The package was also shaped within a worldview which was quite primitive by the standards of the new millennium, whether we consider the worldview of the first centuries of Christian history, the Middle Ages, or of the nineteenth century. Scripture was understood and interpreted in a literalist fashion, as if God personally dictated every word and every event happened exactly as recorded. These factors contributed to producing a very stable, systematized package that held together well and provided a cohesive religious worldview for Catholics. The diagram to the right illustrates some of the elements of this package and its influences.

WORLDVIEW/COSMOLOGY
CHURCH AT CENTER OF SOCIETY
CHURCH AUTHORITY UNQUESTIONED
LITERALIST UNDERSTANDING OF SCRIPTURE

Original Sin
Fall-Redemption
Heaven "Up," Hell "Below"
Gates Of Heaven Locked
Purgatory • Limbo • Indulgences
God • Overseer • Male • Looks Down On Us
God Is Everywhere • God Loves • God Judges
Jesus Is Human • Jesus Is God • Jesus Saves Us
One True Religion • One Way To Heaven
Mary: Queen Of Heaven • Dispenser Of All Graces
Rosary • Novenas • Benediction • Devotions
Papal Authority • Role Of Laity • Baptism
Confirmation • Eucharist • Marriage
Anointing • Confession • Reconciliation
Mortal And Venial Sin • Sexuality
Morality • Divorce
Sunday Obligation

In our lifetime there have been dramatic changes. The church no longer holds center stage; people in western society readily question authority; our understanding of planet Earth's place in the universe has changed, and with it our knowledge about its age and the way life developed here. Scripture scholarship now provides us with different ways of understanding and interpreting Scripture. Historical scholarship reveals to us that some beliefs and practices we thought went back to the time of Jesus and the apostles appeared only in the Middle Ages or even later. Now the "package" seems to be under attack, and, indeed, the factors mentioned above have had an extraordinary impact on Catholic life since Vatican II.

We face a choice. We can immerse ourselves in the "package" and try to fight off all the influences that could persuade us to modify or radically change our beliefs and practices. Or, we can educate ourselves to understand and be conversant with key influences that impinge on our faith, then engage in the challenging task of deepening our appreciation of what we believe in the light of these influences.

We need to appreciate that our contemporary questions about God, Jesus, the church, ourselves, and what we look for in church authority and leadership have their roots both outside of as well as inside the church.

For many adult Catholics, the reforms of Vatican II, as well as the Vietnam War and the church's ruling against contraception, shattered a prided sense of uniformity of belief and practice. These events occurred in the context of western culture questioning blind obedience to authority and urging individuals to take personal responsibility for decisions affecting their lives. For a significant number of Catholics, these events and influences triggered an unheralded response: a refusal to keep giving unquestioning obedience to church authority; an insistence on using their own reasoning to reexamine in searching ways the religious worldview in which they had been nourished; the desire to be treated as adults capable of accepting responsibility. They were also prepared to cast off the fear (often the consequence of Catholic theology) that had prevented them from being assertive, and they demonstrated their willingness to walk away from the established forms of Catholic ritual and religious practice if these were not relevant to their life's journey.

Gallup polls in America have recorded this extraordinary shift in adult American Catholic attitudes and practices: 70 percent of those surveyed think being a good Catholic is not dependent on going to Mass every Sunday. In 1987, 79 percent opposed the papal prohibition on artificial birth control; in 1992, that had risen to 87 percent. Seventy-four percent believe that divorced and remarried Catholics should be able to remain Catholics "in good standing." In 1971, 49 percent approved of married clergy; by 1987 the approval had risen to 70 percent. In 1992, 90 percent of American Catholics believed that someone could dissent from church doctrine and still remain a good Catholic.[1]

Some Catholics would say these surveys simply reflect a period of sad decline from solid church teaching. The Spirit of God could not be saying anything valid here! Things have got out of hand; it is time to recapture and harness the horse that has bolted!

But it is not as simple as that.

The retired archbishop of San Francisco, John Quinn, in an address at Oxford University on June 29, 1996, spoke of the "new situation" in the church today,

> ...shaped by the shattering of the Berlin wall and the collapse of the communist dictatorships, by the awakening of China and her movement into the political and economic world of the 20th century, by the movement toward unification in Europe, by a new and spreading consciousness of the dignity of women, by the arrival of an immense cultural diversity in the church, by the insistent thirst for unity among Christians. This new situation is not only political, economic, cultural and technological. It is marked as well by a new psychology. People think differently, react differently, have new aspirations, a new sense of what is possible, new hopes and dreams. In the church there is a new consciousness of the dignity conferred by baptism and the responsibility for the mission of the church rooted in baptism.[2]

There is no way we can turn a blind eye and pretend these factors do not profoundly affect religious belief and practice.

The task today, being mindful of and realistic about these influences, is to help people converse with one another and share the convictions and the questions they have about God, Jesus, the church, themselves, their religious worldview, and their bonding with the rest of creation.

Some aspects of this task are clear: helping Catholics re-image and re-language some of the basics of their faith; providing a cohesive religious worldview that is in harmony with a contemporary understanding of our place in the universe; introducing adult Catholics to some of the insights of contemporary Scripture scholarship; examining the relationship of Christianity with other world religions; and articulating and promoting a spirituality which energizes, encourages, and challenges.

The work of adult faith development is obviously of major importance here in attempting to bridge the gap between scholarship and the faith understanding of all believers. Adult faith educators are bridge builders: they listen, engage, converse, present information, challenge, and open doors in the hope that people will step in and continue to search and deepen their faith. Hopefully, this book will assist in that task.

The book has five main goals:

• first, to help Catholics and other Christians develop a sense of awesome wonder about the God in whom they believe;

• second, to help them better appreciate the place of Jesus in human affairs;

• third, to help them realize that the same Spirit of God that moved in Jesus moves in all of us;

• fourth, to take that last statement really seriously, and to consider how it challenges all of us to be the presence of God in the world today;

• fifth, to explore the type of church leadership and authority we look for in a new millennium.

A broader intent is to accomplish this within a framework or worldview that is cohesive and makes sense to the modern mind. The

content must be able to stand up to the rigorous questioning prevalent today about any religious worldview. It must engage present scientific understanding about our place in the universe, the development of life on this planet, the connectedness of all people with one
another and with life on this planet, and the reality of a God who is
in all, with all, and through all.

Underlying all these goals is a very simple desire: to get people
talking about what they believe, why they believe what they believe,
what are the foundations of their belief system, and what are the
deeper questions of faith and meaning they may never have articulat-
ed for themselves before. The years of working in adult faith formation have convinced me that young adults, the middle-aged, and the
elderly find themselves engrossed in stimulating and rewarding conversation when issues of faith are approached this way.

A major concern with this book is to communicate with the reader in simple language—an approach which has its advantages and
inherent disadvantages. But if the task of adult faith development is
to engage people's experiences and questions, present information
for reflection and discussion, and so develop understanding and
growth in faith and commitment, that task requires simple language
if it is to involve as many people as possible.

Each chapter ends with some questions for reflection and/or discussion. Several chapters also offer a brief recommended reading list.
The main criterion for recommending a book (apart from the obvious fact that its matter is worthwhile) is that it be simple enough to
read. Readers wanting more technical resources are referred to the
Notes and the Bibliography.

The word "church" refers to the Catholic Church, but this usage is
in no way desired or intended to limit the reality of "church" to the
Catholic Church. While parts of the book are particularly focused on
the Catholic Church, much of it is applicable to all Christian churches.

NOTES

1. Fries, Heinrich, *Suffering From the Church* (Collegeville, MN: The Liturgical Press, 1995). The survey appears in a Foreword by Leonard Swidler, pp. 12–13.

2. Quinn, John, "Considering the Papacy," in *Origins*, July 18, 1996, vol. 28, no. 8, p. 120.

CHAPTER ONE

Our Images of God

The way we image or imagine what "God" is like forms the foundation of our religious beliefs. Changes in our image inevitably force changes to our way of thinking about God, about ourselves, and about ourselves in relationship with God. An obvious case is if we were to change from imagining God as a strict judge, ready to punish, to being a compassionate, merciful, infinitely loving God. Such a change in our image would almost certainly lead to a change in the way we would pray, worship, and see ourselves in relationship with God—all of which in turn would surely lessen fear and lead to greater peace of mind.

Each of us could probably recall times in our lives when we have been led to change our image of God in some way. Most of us could also mention searching questions we are still asking about the way we image God. "Why?" questions come quickly to mind. Why doesn't God do this or that? Why does God let this or that happen? The questions we ask are very much bound up with the way we imagine God to be.

Four points stand out clearly when we begin to examine in a thorough manner the way we image God:

1. We are on dangerous ground! There will certainly be a domino effect if we change in any significant way our image of God. The effect will be not only on our personal faith and prayer, but ultimately our belief and worship will change on many levels.

2. We *must* tackle the task. We can no longer afford to carry around images of God that are based on a worldview that no longer reflects reality. Examining how one particular worldview fashioned many of the prevailing images of God will be one of the key steps in the task before us. We have to be able to provide images of God and speak about God in ways that are relevant to today's worldview.

3. We will still be left with questions. We will never fully understand the ultimate mystery that is God, a mystery beyond our comprehension. But hopefully, there will be a profound and significant shift in the nature of our questions, reflecting a more thoughtful image of God.

4. Whatever we do in examining our images of God and in talking about God, we need to remind ourselves constantly that we are not *describing* God; at best we are using images and thoughts that grasp at insights. With these images and thoughts we build a mental model of what God is like. We need to be wary of supposing that our mental model is actually what God is.

One of the biggest problems we encounter when we reflect on what God is like is the tension between two opposite poles. On the one hand, God is the reality that is utterly beyond anything we can describe or imagine, unimaginably intelligent, having no need for nor dependent on anything created, able to exist solely without any created reality. So we speak of God being "transcendent" (literally, rising above, passing beyond, surmounting).

On the other hand, God is *everywhere*. Everything that has existence is permeated with the presence of this divine reality. God can be "seen" and "known" in the beauty and wonder of creation; God is "love" and when we live in love we live in God. God is compassionate, merciful, concerned, forgiving—these are all basic insights we glean from Scripture. That is to say, the reality we name as "God" is here with, involved with, intimately connected with human experience, and indeed, connected intimately with everything that exists. So we speak of God being "immanent," which literally means actually present or abiding in.

There are pitfalls on both ends of the pole.

The transcendent aspect of God can come to be understood in a way that emphasizes spatial distance rather than a reality that is beyond our comprehension and our images and language. When that happens, the image of God gets locked into the distant God, the God distinct from us who fits the overseer image so prevalent in popular Christian thinking and imagination. This is the God who, as it were, clicks the fingers and creation starts off, then God sits back and watches it unfold, all according to a plan in God's infinite intelligence, intervening now and then, sometimes in response to our prayer. In popular thinking God is "out there," watching over, "looking down" on us.

As we will see, this image of God blended well with a cosmology (the study of the universe as a system and our place in it) that understood Earth to be at the center of the universe. It is easy to see how religions working within a primitive cosmology came to image God (or the gods) living above the clouds, looking down on Earth. The dwelling place of evil spirits in these thought patterns was usually somewhere below us, in the underworld: up to heaven, down to hell. Consider how strong that simple religious cosmology has been in shaping our images of God.

Alternatively, the immanent aspect of God can be so stressed that we end up with God being tied to, locked into creation, as if there were no greater dimension to God's reality. This ultimately leads to an image of God being no greater than the sum total of creation.

We need to keep an eye on both poles as we explore our image of God, our understanding of God's creative activity, and our relationship with God.

POPULAR CHRISTIAN RELIGIOUS WORLDVIEW

Let us examine the way many Christians imagine God relating with the first human beings and the way this in turn shapes their image of God. We go to the story of Adam and Eve in the second account of creation in the book of Genesis. This story shaped the religious worldview for many of us. Whether we now take the story as literally true or not is not the issue here (but we shall return to it as an issue later); our focus here is simply on the way the story has led people to image human beings' basic relationship with God. Here follows a summary of this account:

God created human beings in God's own image and in the beginning they were closely acquainted with God. Adam and Eve came into "paradise." They had dominion over all creation. But pride and disobedience caused them to do wrong. God reacted to their sin. Adam and Eve were driven out of the Garden of Eden; they lost paradise. They would now have to endure death.

Women had their own particular punishment:

> I will greatly increase your pangs in childbearing; in pain you shall bring forth children, yet your desire shall be for your husband, and he shall rule over you (Gen 3:16).

And men had theirs:

> ...cursed is the ground because of you; in toil you shall eat of it all the days of your life....By the sweat of your face you shall eat bread until you return to the ground, for out of it you were taken; you are dust, and to dust you shall return (Gen 3:17–19).

So human beings became the "poor, banished children of Eve, mourning and weeping in this valley of tears." We lost God's friendship. The gates of heaven were locked.

It is always interesting to participate with a group of middle-aged or older Catholics who are sharing the images of this worldview, which they acquired as children, and their understanding of what followed in the story. The sharing is usually along these lines: the souls of all who died after Adam and Eve could not go to heaven. Many imagined a dark underworld place—the Limbo of the patriarchs was a name given to this "place"—where all the souls went and waited, and waited. Then Jesus came, "saved" them—and us—and by his suffering and death, won back God's friendship, and opened the gates of heaven. We learned in the Apostles' Creed that "he descended into hell, and on the third day he rose again." These words helped to shape our image of the millions of souls waiting and waiting, and of the "Alleluias" that must have been uttered when Jesus came and they rose with him into heaven at last.

From the Adam and Eve story we inherited images that have emphasized the distant God—the God who withdrew from us, the God who closed the gates. When this story went hand in hand with a primitive cosmology it is not surprising that images of God in heaven looking down on us were cemented in our minds. As the diagram below suggests, we are on Earth and God is above, in heaven. Our prayer, for example, goes "up" to God.

We have rarely been encouraged to reflect on the lasting impression and the deeply etched images the popular understanding of the story of Adam and Eve have formed within our psyche. What are some of its more influential, lasting, and questionable effects on the way many people have come to imagine God and our relationship with God?

First, God is viewed as a being in our likeness. In the creation story, God walked around the garden; God carried on a conversation. Then, because of the sin of Adam and Eve, God withdrew from them. We then carry with us the image of God as "person." Yes, we may say God is infinite, God is everywhere, God is not an old man in the sky; but the prevailing image of God is still that of a Supreme Person localized somewhere out there or up there, someone who hears and reacts much like a human person hears and reacts. This "localizing" of God has had a powerful influence on the image of God as the "overseer" and the fact that God is imaged as being male. Our male language about God, "he" doing this or that, cements the image of a particular being in space who listens and reacts.

This image of a God who takes offense at human wrongdoing and reacts, who listens and responds, permeates the general Christian attitude to prayer. Take, for example, a prayer such as, "O my God, I am heartily sorry for having offended you...." To whom and where is a prayer like that addressed? To a male, localized God in outer space? What does it mean to suggest that God is "offended" by our sin? Does God somewhere-out-there react and want to punish our sin? Sin *is* real; its effects are harmful. But God reacting and locking us out of heaven? What validity do such images have? How are we imaging God when we engage in this type of discussion?

All this has consequences for the way we think about Jesus and his role. We will see more of this later. How are we to understand language such as "Jesus came to save us"? From where did he come? What do we imagine caused him to come? Many of us were led to imagine a scene in heaven in which God the Father said to the Son something like, "Son, I gave human beings everything and they messed it up. They are not capable of making up to me for the enormous offense they have given, so you had best go down and live the human life as I have wanted it lived. I will then relent, and give them my friendship again, and allow them to come into heaven with us." So the life and death of Jesus was understood as effecting *a change of attitude within God.*

From this viewpoint, we acquired an understanding of salvation as being primarily concerned with "getting to heaven" or "saving our souls." For many centuries much of the church's missionary effort and self-understanding was driven by this same understanding and concern.

For ourselves, personally, we took on enormous guilt. As impressionable children we learned that God was good, God gave us paradise—and we blew it! We failed. We are the cause of death and disaster. We deserve punishment.

What an image of ourselves!

Many of us will recognize in the following statements ideas and attitudes we acquired from the story of the "fall" of Adam and Eve.

• God is all-powerful; God can do anything; God is "perfect"; God cannot change.

• God created our world with living things in perfect harmony.

• Human beings are the cause of death.

• God created, and creation unfolds with God standing back, as it were, watching it unfold according to God's plan.

• God decides what will happen to us in life. God decides, for example, when we will die. We speak of accepting "God's will."

• God can change the weather if we pray hard enough.

• Death will be our meeting time with God; God will judge us; heaven is a place; so is hell.

• God is not close to us; saintly people are the exception because they do great and wonderful deeds.

While this religious worldview may have been adequate for the past 2,000 years, it has become increasingly indefensible in the face of contemporary understanding of the universe and its development.

The challenges to this religious worldview which shaped many of us as Christians are enormous and must be faced squarely if our language about God is to be relevant at the end of the twentieth century. Some of the challenges we must deal with are:

• Human beings did not come into paradise. Disasters and catastrophes of gigantic proportions were part and parcel of this planet's reality long, long before human beings came into existence.

• Death *did not* come into the world through human sin. Again, it was a reality millions and millions of years before human beings walked the planet.

• God is not localized somewhere. God's reality is of an infinite nature. God is everywhere.

• The image of a God figure reacting against us.

• God's responsibility for an inevitably "imperfect," limited creation.

• The fact that Jesus, in his ministry, did not act out of any awareness whatsoever that the poor, the outcasts, the sinners, whoever, had lost God's friendship. In fact, it was quite the opposite. He wanted people to rid themselves (turn from, convert) any ideas, attitudes, or religious practices that suggested God was not close to them in an unconditional, loving way. Jesus was clearly not concerned with changing any attitude within God. He was very clearly focused on people changing their wrong images of God. There is an enormous challenge here to the way Christians generally think about Jesus and his role as "savior." How are we to understand "salvation" and Jesus' role in it?

These ideas will be treated more fully in the pages to follow.

One of the fundamental issues is God's involvement in creation; not just that God created, but the issue of God's connectedness (or disconnectedness) with what came into being. Are we to imagine God as the Super Being who creates then stands back from what has been created, watching "over" it? Late last century, the First Vatican Council in its Dogmatic Constitution, *Dei Filius* (On the Catholic Faith), made this statement at the beginning of its first chapter, "God, Creator of All Things":

> As He is one unique and spiritual substance, entirely simple and unchangeable, we must proclaim Him distinct from the world in existence and essence, blissful in Himself and from Himself, ineffably exalted above all things that exist....[1]

The statement has to be read in the context of the time. The church was defending the concept of God from what it saw as pantheistic movements—reducing God to nature worship. But in rightly defending the transcendence of God the statement makes it difficult to get away from the image of a "person" (he, him), "distinct from the world," "unchangeable."

Unchangeable? If ever an attribute of God needed close examination it is surely this one. Why can't God change? The traditional philosophical answer has been because God is perfect and perfection by definition rules out any need to change to something different. At the very least there is a huge problem here if we are to hold at the same time that God is compassionate, feels with, responds to, and is involved in the unfolding universe.

This highlights one of the problems we have in imagining what God is like. We keep bumping into the two poles mentioned earlier: the transcendence and the immanence of God. This can be helpful for us, rather than a constant stumbling block, because it alerts us to the dangers of making absolute statements about God. Transcendence basically means that God is beyond any statement we can make about God. We have to be able to hold the mystery: yes, God is distinct from, other than, not identified by the created universe; and, yes, God is concerned, involved with, intimately connected to, moved by the created universe.

The challenge is whether we can appreciate the reality and the mystery of these two dimensions of God, and at the same time speak meaningfully about this God in relation to our universe and ourselves in the light of today's understanding of the universe (cosmos) and our place in it. What is certain is that the old cosmology has gone and with it many of our religious images: Earth as the center of creation; heaven is "up," and so is God; hell is "below," and so is the devil; God is distinct, apart from us, looking down on us; the beginning of life on this planet characterized by peace and harmony—paradise.

What we then discover is that even slight changes to our thinking and imaging here will influence a significant portion of our religious language. We Christians need to re-image and re-language the basic truths that were packaged in the old cosmology; otherwise, our Christian religious worldview will be seen as an irrelevant museum piece in a world that is rethinking its place in the universe.

Believing that God is actively present *everywhere* in our world and in our universe, can we tell a story about God and our relationship with God which encompasses this reality? And if we can, the next challenge is how to read our Scriptures and how to understand Jesus, human and divine, and ourselves who share the same spirit of Jesus in the light of this story.

Will we, can we, tell a story about the God who is within and through all, a God who is embodied in all that has life, a God who emerges in a wonderful fashion in human beings? Or will we continue to tell a story about a distant overseer God, a "fall" that separated us from God's love and presence, ourselves as "poor, banished children of Eve, mourning and weeping in this valley of tears," and a Jesus whose role it is to change God's mind by his suffering and death?

The challenge may be daunting for most of us, as Christians, to face. But in facing it we may discover a God greater and more life-giving, more freeing and more infinitely loving than we have ever imagined. This reason alone will make exploring the questions worthwhile.

The challenge invites us to break new ground. When we encounter the challenge we find we are shaking some of the foundations of our religious belief system, disturbing long-held, cherished beliefs and images. For some people this can cause confusion and lead to many questions, but this need not be a negative experience. Conversion of mind and heart rarely happens if we are not firstly disturbed from our usual patterns of thinking. Jesus disturbed people this way.

NOTES

1. Neuner, J. and Dupuis J., *The Christian Faith: Doctrinal Documents of the Catholic Church*, 5th & enlarged ed. (London: HarperCollins Religious, 1992), p. 120.

2. Birch, Charles, *On Purpose* (Sydney: New South Wales University Press, Ltd., 1990), pp. 88-89.

REFLECTION

- Where am I being challenged?
- What are the questions I have about my images of God?
- In what ways do I think in and act out of the traditional model of myself in relation with God?
- How does it influence my prayer? How has it in the past?
- How do I view creation and God's activity in it?
- What are my reactions to the following passage?

There are many concepts of God and many of them should die.

The primary question is not, do you believe in God? but, what do you think you would be believing in if you did believe in God? There is the God who can do anything, who could prevent nuclear war, who could have prevented the holocaust—but didn't. There is the God who set the universe going in the first place and then left it except for occasional interventions in the form of miracles which rarely happen. There is the God of the gaps who is brought in to fill the gaps left by science; that God grows smaller with every advance in scientific understanding of the universe. There is the cosmic bellhop who sits at the end of a cosmic telephone exchange dealing with billions of calls every minute and whom the caller hopes will alter the course of events to suit the caller. There is the God who requires praise. There is the God who demands sacrifice. There is the God who is on our side in wars who would have us kill for his sake. There is the uncertain God of the soldier's prayer—please God, if there be a God, save my soul if there be a soul! There is the God of judgment who rules by fear and who dispenses post-mortem rewards and punishments. All these theologies of God make things pretty easy for atheists.[2]

CHAPTER TWO

Our Changing Worldview

Theology is the study of God and God's connectedness with life and the universe. Theology is never done in a vacuum. It is always pursued within a context of time, place, culture, and worldview. There are different worldviews from which people can view reality and these worldviews influence the way people image God, their connectedness with God, and the way they respond in prayer, worship, ritual, and behavior.

A difficulty arises when theology becomes so tied to a particular worldview or understanding of the universe that its statements come under threat of being irrelevant if there is a dramatic shift in worldview or cosmology. The classic case is Galileo. When Galileo asserted that the Earth *moves* and is not the center of the universe, church authorities condemned him. In fairness to church authorities of the time it should be noted that Galileo had strong critics in the scientific world also, and some of them used church influence to discredit him: the scientific world is not exactly innocent in this affair!

Nor was Galileo himself simply an innocent victim of repression. His sharp tongue did not help his cause in the face of opposition.

However, the fact is that in old age Galileo was formally accused of heresy because his teaching contradicted Scripture. At the age of seventy, Galileo, a desperately sick man, was carried on a stretcher in the midst of winter from Florence to Rome, summoned there by the pope. Some months later, on Wednesday, June 22, 1633, he was publicly humiliated and disgraced when church authorities forced him to declare:

> ...after an injunction had been lawfully intimated to me by this Holy Office to the effect that I must altogether abandon the false opinion...that the Earth is not the center of the world and moves, and that I must not hold, defend or teach, in any way, verbally or in writing, the said false doctrine, and after it had been notified to me that the said doctrine was contrary to Holy Scripture...I have been judged to be vehemently suspected of heresy...I abjure, curse, and detest the aforesaid errors and heresies...and I swear that in the future I will never again say or assert verbally or in writing anything that might cause a similar suspicion....[1]

This incident in our church's history is a classic example of protection of doctrine (i.e., officially sanctioned teaching to be believed) or of a particular way of understanding Scripture refusing to consider that reality could be different from the way church hierarchy perceived it to be. Church authority's insistence on protecting doctrine and Scripture, which they thought depended on a particular cosmology, meant that ears and eyes and minds were closed to considerations and facts that would force modifications to the way doctrine might be expressed or Scripture understood.

It took 350 years for the Catholic Church to offer the scientific world—and the world in general—an apology for its treatment of Galileo. We would, should, expect that this same sort of mistake would not be made again. There is evidence, though, that the church today in its teaching authority is ambiguous in its approach to adaptation of its teaching to contemporary thought. The Second Vatican Council demonstrated a willingness to engage the challenge and gave great encouragement to renewal and updating. But the opinion of many Catholics who engage in adult faith formation programs is that their church, not only in Rome but on many levels, seems painfully reluctant to meet the challenge of expressing traditional faith in the language, images, and worldview of contemporary society.

If our faith is to be relevant as well as strong, we need to familiarize ourselves with the worldview or cosmology that is taken for granted today, a worldview in which today's children are being educated, a worldview quite different from that in which traditional Christian faith was shaped. It is in this worldview that we are being challenged to speak about God, Jesus, church, and our Christian faith with cohesion and vitality. Michael Dowd expresses the challenge well:

> If a people's cosmology or creation story is their foundation for all meaning and value and if our present chaos is due to the fact that we live and operate within institutions that are founded on a cosmology that does not correspond to reality, then learning this new cosmology and its meaning would certainly seem to be important for Christians to do. Moreover, if this cosmology is a revelation of God, if it is the truth about the nature of Reality, then not only will it not contradict the truth of Christianity, it will open up its deeper meanings and unleash its transforming, prophetic power.[2]

Let us then explore the new cosmology and its implications for us today. We start with a caution: what follows is not the final scientific word on the beginning or the development of the universe and our planet. Scientific knowledge will undoubtedly increase. For the present we are simply trying to engage the generally accepted broad view of contemporary scientific knowledge.

Sallie McFague provides this summary in her book, *The Body of God*:

In the beginning, the universe was infinitely hot and infinitely condensed. In their study of what happened right at the beginning, scientists now claim to have worked back to within 10 to the minus

35 of the first second of the beginning of the universe. That is this much of a second:

.000000000000000000000000000000000001.

(It boggles the imagination to consider how much more precise scientists will claim to be in their knowledge of the first second in, say, five hundred years' time!)

In the *first second* the temperature fell to ten thousand million degrees. That is about one thousand times hotter than the center of the sun. In the next one and a half minutes the temperature dropped nine thousand million degrees. Protons and neutrons combined to produce helium and hydrogen in what could be described as universal nuclear reactions. This production stopped after three minutes when there was not enough heat present to sustain the reactions.

The universe continued to cool and expand. Atoms began to form when cooling over more than millions of years dropped the temperature to a few thousand degrees. The force of gravity then condensed matter into the first stars and galaxies. Nuclear reactions started up again in the interior of this first generation of stars.

> These stars eventually produced a second generation when they collapsed through a tremendous explosion (a supernova) spewing out the heavier elements of carbon and iron, elements essential for life. Our sun is a second- or third-generation star, formed about five billion years ago from debris of the supernovas....[3]

Another scientist, Brian Swimme, gives a fascinating description of the way our ability to read the words on a page is dependent on and connected with those fireballs at the beginning of time. Paraphrased, Swimme presents this picture:

> As you are reading this page electricity is flowing through your nervous system. On this flow depends all your thinking, your sensations, emotions, and, in fact, your very aliveness. Ions in the brain ebb and flow as part of this movement, but do not move of their own accord; they have to be stimulated and it is

energy-soaked molecules in the brain which do this. The molecules get their energy from the food you eat. In turn the food received its energy from the sun. Of vital importance are the photons which the food receives from the sun because it is these photons, photonic energy, that create the movement of the ions in your brain at this very instant.

The sun produces the photons in its core, where atomic fusion creates helium atoms out of hydrogen atoms and in the process, photons are released in sunlight.

What is most remarkable about all this is that you can trace the process back: the ions in the brain depending on food, the food dependent on photons produced in the core of the sun, the sun resulting from previous "supernova" explosions when stars exploded and all of this resulting from and a participation in whatever happened in the first moment of the beginning of this universe.

Swimme concludes this section,

...and this photonic shower from the beginning of time powers your thinking.... Fires from the beginning of time empower you *right now—this instant.* What you are thinking and feeling this very moment is possible only through the cosmic fire. Your entire nervous system is rich in this fire.[4]

It is no wonder McFague, at the end of her summary, quotes J. Polkinghorne's graphic and poetic words, "We are all made from the ashes of dead stars."

It is generally considered that the universe is about 15 billion years old. Being in touch with 15 billion years of activity is mind-boggling! The grace we need today may well be that a sense of wonder be born anew in us as we contemplate the reality of our place in the universe. Swimme captures something of that wonder in this passage:

The primeval fireball existed for twenty billion years without self-awareness. The creative work of the supernovas existed for billions of years without self-reflective awareness. That star could not, by itself, become aware of its own beauty or sacrifice. But the star can, through us, reflect back on itself. In a sense, you are the star....

You *are* that star, brought into a form of life that enables life to reflect on itself. So, yes, the star *does* know of its great work, of its surrender to allurement, of its stupendous contribution to life, but only through its further articulation—you.

When you take the story of the universe as your basic referent, all your thoughts and actions are different.[5]

This is an awesome, wonder-full, uplifting, "wow!" approach to human existence and our place in this universe. This is a different story about who we are, and its magnificence and grandeur have the capacity to call us into a new consciousness about the response we humans give to life and the respect we give to the rest of creation.

When we consider the development of the universe and our place in it, our sense of wonder cannot fail to be awakened. When we move on to consider the size of the universe, we should give our sense of wonder full rein, for we are now in the realm of an awesome reality, totally beyond our imagination.

IMMENSITY OF THE UNIVERSE

Just inside the door of the visitors' center at the space radio telescope situated outside Parkes, New South Wales, Australia, is a list of statistics designed to move people to wonder at the size of our galaxy, the Milky Way. One item suggests that we imagine the sun and its planets, i.e., our solar system, represented on a scale the size of a postage stamp. Using the same scale, it asks what area would we need to depict the rest of the Milky Way. The answer: an area the size of Australia (or the United States of America). Imagine it! Put a postage stamp on the ground: on that scale even the smallest dot on the stamp would be too big to represent our planet Earth. Compare the dot on this stamp with an area the size of Australia and we have an idea of how insignificant Earth is in this galaxy.

Any encyclopedia will provide a wealth of wonder-full information on our galaxy and its place in the universe. For example,

• There are more than 200 billion stars in this one galaxy.

• Our galaxy is so wide that light, traveling at 300,000 kilometers a second, takes 100,000 years to cross it.

• The sun with its planets travels around this galaxy at a speed of 210 kilometers *a second*. One trip around the galaxy takes 250 million years![6]

Our minds have enough difficulty trying to cope with just this one galaxy! It is only since the 1920s that scientists came to know of other galaxies and they are still in the infancy stages of exploring the rest of our universe. Close to home, as it were, we know the Milky Way is the second biggest galaxy in a cluster of 30 galaxies. The biggest galaxy in the cluster is Andromeda. It is a mere 18,921,600,000,000,000,000 kilometers from us. Its diameter is in the region of 1,229,904,000,000,000,000 kilometers.[7]

How many galaxies are out there?

Astronomers now estimate that there are more than *three hundred billion* galaxies, each with billions and billions and billions of stars. Furthermore, it is considered that the universe is expanding and the further away galaxies are from one another, the greater the speed of expansion.

As if all this isn't enough to boggle our minds completely, scientists are now wondering whether there might not be *many* universes! John Gribbin (astrophysicist and physics consultant for *New Scientist* magazine) comments on recent discoveries: "together...discoveries have led to the idea that our universe is just one among a multitude of universes, and that in some sense the many universes are competing with one another for the right to exist."[8]

What does all this information about our universe do to our image of God? Each of us has to answer that for ourselves. At the very least our contemplation of the vastness and the wonder, the sheer awesomeness of our universe might put us in touch with the necessity of being "expansive" in our image of God. At the same time we might be more wary of the ways we have "boxed" God, localized God, and limited God within the confines of our images. In colloquial terms, can we allow our image of God "to blow our minds"? Can we try to grasp the smallest insight, in wonder and awe, into the immensity of with whom and with what we are dealing when we try to image the reality we name as "God"? Will we stop putting God into the straitjacket of our small minds and images and allow God to be God—whatever that may be for God?

Even if someone wants to object that the idea of many universes is simply scientific theory, the point remains: is our image of God capable of dealing with the theory? Or will we dig in our heels, as in the Galileo affair, and say this concept cannot possibly be entertained because it does not fit in with our theological notions?

Let us pause and consider how this new worldview challenges some of our images of God and ways we think of ourselves in relationship with God.

If God is truly everywhere, even to the limitless vastness of the cosmos and beyond, where does my prayer go when I pray to God? What, who, am I imagining "hears" or "listens to" my prayer? Can and will I think about this, wrestle with the challenge of the questions, and engage the wonder of relationship with Immense Awesomeness and Immense Mystery?

Whatever God is, God is surely not a localized person (as we understand "person") up in the sky somewhere. We will want to affirm that God is personal, but we will have to be more careful in understanding and imaging what that means. The tendency has been to image God as a person like us, so the image of God has taken on a male, localized aspect. Our mistake has been to take *relational* images of trust, e.g., "Father," and make them descriptions of God; they are not that.

It is extremely difficult to break out of the male, localized syndrome, the more so because it is so pervasive in church language, in liturgy, and in popular prayer and devotion. Our constant use of "he" language about God only serves to cement images of a localized being in outer space.

What does it mean to believe that this infinite, "personal" reality that I name "God" really, actually loves me, personally? Where do I engage the "personal" aspect of this God? If "heaven" is wherever God is, what happens to our images and ideas about heaven in light of contemporary cosmology?

We can begin to see, hopefully, that our contemporary perceptions of our place in the universe influence our religious worldview and images. Some of these, in turn, will inevitably be different from those of our ancestors. Their worldview made it easy for them to believe in a localized, male God up in heaven, who looked down on and looked after life on our planet. When we now take a step further and reflect on the development of life on Earth, we engage more issues and data which challenge popular images of God and the way many Christians image their connectedness with God.

LIFE ON EARTH

Primary school children today can go to their library, take out an encyclopedia, and find the following time chart for life on Earth. They take this for granted as the way life developed on Earth. They learn, give or take a few million years here and there, that our universe came into existence about fifteen billion years ago, that our solar system formed about five billion years ago, and that life forms developed on our planet in this progression:

• Three and a half billion years: the oldest fossils (from Western Australia) come from this time.

• Two billion years: oxygen in the atmosphere; breathing possible.

• Seven hundred million years: soft-bodied animals.

• Six hundred million years: shelled, skeletal forms of life.

• Five hundred million years: fish.

• Four hundred and fifty million years: plants.

• Four hundred million years: insects.

• Two hundred and fifty million years: earliest reptiles; conifers.

• Two hundred and twenty million years: mammals appear.

• Two hundred and five million years: the late Triassic Period; dinosaurs.

- One hundred and thirty million years: first flowering plants.
- Sixty-five million years: dinosaurs extinct.
- Sixty million years: primates; forest horses.
- Twenty million years: grassland animals.
- Ten million years: mammals reach height of diversity.
- Four million years: southern ape *(Australopithecus)*.
- Two million years: *homo erectus*; used fire and tools.
- One million, eight hundred thousand years: great Ice Age; massive, sudden change to ecology worldwide; widespread extinction of species; survivors were mainly the smaller species.
- Three hundred thousand years: *homo sapiens*; Neanderthals.
- Thirty thousand years: *homo sapiens sapiens*.[9]

We need not get into a debate about whether we descended from apes or not (though it is likely primary children will not have the resistance many adults have to considering this). The point of the time chart is simply to show two things: development from simple life forms to more complex life forms is an accepted fact in today's worldview; and human beings are very, very late arrivals on the world scene. There have been several efforts to depict just how late is our arrival on the scene by imagining the history of the universe on a scale of one year. Michael Dowd presents this view:

> If we imagine that our 15 billion year history was compressed into a single year:
>
> The Milky Way galaxy self-organized in late February; our solar system emerged from the elemental stardust of an exploded supernova in early September; the planetary oceans formed in mid-September; Earth awakened into life in late September; sex was invented in late November; the dinosaurs lived for a few days in early December; flowering plants burst upon the scene with a dazzling array of color mid-December; and the universe began reflecting consciously in and through the human, with choice and free will, less than ten minutes before midnight on December 31st....
>
> We have known we are in fact the Earth thinking about itself for only the last few seconds.[10]

On this scale of 12 months, Jesus would be born on December 31st at 11:59:45 PM. The major scientific discoveries of this century would be in the final second before the end of the year.

In the contemporary scientific worldview we are latecomers to this planet. Not only are we latecomers, we are totally dependent on an ecological system that nurtured us very slowly into existence. We came into existence through a long process of adaptations, changes, and upheavals in the development of life on this planet.

It is not surprising that church authority so strongly resisted this scientific understanding of the development of life. Much of Christian theology depended on a worldview which held that human beings came into paradise and things went wrong because of human beings. What happens now when we are confronted with over-whelming evidence that development, death, disaster, and upheaval were part and parcel of this planet's existence millions and millions of years before human beings entered the scene? What happens when primary school children are educated to a totally different worldview and learn, for example, that dinosaurs became extinct more than sixty-three million years before human beings came into existence? What happens when the images of God that have been so ingrained in us, still so much a part of our religious thinking and practice, are brought into question by different ways of viewing creation, the universe, reality?

What happens, for example, with the deeply entrenched doctrine of original sin linked as it is to a literal understanding of Creation and the Fall? What if there wasn't a "fall" anything like what was described in the book of Genesis? How, then, do we speak meaningfully about the reality of sin, our connectedness with the divine, the life of Jesus, and the reality of Jesus being savior for us?

SYMBOLIC VS. LITERAL

It is generally agreed that the story of the fall of Adam and Eve is myth. Unfortunately, in the popular mind, "myth" is associated with fairy-tale or make-believe that can be readily dismissed. Myth, however, can not be easily discarded. It is the endeavor of human beings to plumb the depths of mystery, to find insights into the deepest questions of life and life's meaning and purpose. Beyond the story, beyond the "symbol," people are trying to express profound insights, and they will derive meaning and direction for personal and communal life from the mythical story.

The creation stories in Genesis have extraordinary religious insights: a God who creates freely and lavishly; human beings in close friendship with God; human beings created in God's own image; human beings in connectedness with the rest of creation. The stories reflect on the realities of sin and death, and wonder how these came about and how they connect with the belief in a giving, creating God. They express the belief that we human beings cause harm (sin) because we do not live according to the original designs of God. These myths contain truths and insights that several of the most significant religions in the world live by. They give meaning to who we are.

Myth and symbol can do that when used properly, when due respect is given to their ability to touch us at the deeper levels of meaning, purpose, and our connectedness. Myth and symbol are misunderstood and wrongly used when people cannot move beyond the literal sense, i.e., in believing the story itself has to be factual. So we will find some Christians arguing still that the world was created by God in six days.

It is disappointing to find the *Catechism of the Catholic Church* leaning heavily to a literal interpretation of the Fall. In a resource which Catholics have been urged to consult we find an outmoded worldview which educated people must find difficult to take seriously in light of contemporary scientific knowledge. In the section on Creation and the Fall, the *Catechism* states,

> The account of the fall in Genesis 3 uses figurative language, but affirms a primeval event, a deed that took place *at the beginning of the history of man* (#390).
>
> The harmony in which they had found themselves, thanks to original justice, is now destroyed: the control of the soul's spir-

itual faculties over the body is shattered; the union of man and woman becomes subject to tensions, their relations henceforth marked by lust and domination. Harmony with creation is broken: visible creation has become alien and hostile to man. Because of man, creation is now subject "to its bondage to decay." Finally, the consequence explicitly foretold for this disobedience will come true: man will "return to the ground," for out of it he was taken. *Death makes its entrance into human history* (#400).[11]

Let us be clear and unequivocal: scientifically, this is nonsense. Human beings did not come into a harmonious world. Where is the scientific evidence to show that human beings came into existence with the "spiritual faculties" in control of the body? And to declare that creation became subject to decay "because of man" is an assertion which totally disregards the evidence of millions of years of development of life on the planet before human beings appeared. Were the first human beings on this planet *"explicitly foretold"* anything at all by God?

Why, then, in a catechism published in 1994, do we find this literal approach to a story that Catholic Scripture scholars and scholarship in general advise us not to take literally? The answer becomes clear in #389 of the *Catechism*:

The Church, which has the mind of Christ, knows very well that we cannot tamper with the revelation of original sin without undermining the mystery of Christ.

This implies that the *only* way the church, in its authoritative teaching, has to understand Jesus is in terms of a "fall" taken literally and in insisting on the reality of "paradise" before "man" made creation on this planet "alien and hostile." The fear seems to be that if this (literal story) is not how things happened in the beginning, what do we do with the need for Jesus to come and save us? Searching questions would then arise about "redemption." Why do we need to be "redeemed"? Redeemed from what? Did God, in the form of Jesus, have to come from somewhere else to "save" us?

Is it not possible that the church in its Scriptures and in its tradition has an alternative to the redemption model? Is it not possible that the church could acknowledge the symbolic nature of the Adam and Eve story (and help Christians to read it in this light) and yet not undermine the "mystery of Christ"? Could not (and should not) the *Catechism* and church leadership at all levels try to set us free from images of God and an understanding of Jesus that are dependent on an outdated worldview? Could not (and should not) church leadership engage the reality of contemporary cosmology and help the faithful to do so also?

Granted we answer affirmatively, two further questions become very important. First, are we Christians open to exploring our beliefs in the light of new knowledge and new ways of understanding reality? Second, are we Christians being supported in our church communities, through processes of adult faith education, as we explore our beliefs?

Why would the answer ever be "No!" for either question?

A possible reason for negative responses is a fear that new knowledge will undermine well-established religious thought patterns. It would be a great pity if that fear held sway: first, because new knowledge must be incorporated into our religious worldview, otherwise that worldview becomes outdated and unreal; and second, because it would prevent us developing an even greater sense of awesome wonder in our relationship with God.

Let our God of presence, love, creativity, freedom, and life be beyond our imagination! Let us learn to live in greater awe and wonder as we contemplate and own the contemporary story of human development on planet Earth in this magnificent universe. Let us look more carefully at our response to the gifts of life, intelligence, reason, choice, and love as we contemplate our uniqueness. Let us be more reverent and sensitive towards planet Earth and its life systems which nurtured us into existence. Let us grow in awareness of the mystery of God's presence always sustaining us in existence.

The new cosmology and its worldview are not a threat to

Christianity. In fact, as we shall see in the later chapter on spirituality, a beautiful marriage is possible between this cosmology and the message of Pentecost. Isn't this a truly amazing God in whom we place our faith, in whom we discern purpose in life and who blesses us so richly with God's Spirit, always at work in creation?

NOTES

1. Boorstin, Daniel J., *The Discoverers: A History of Man's Search to Know His World and Himself* (New York: Vintage Books, 1985), p. 326.

2. Dowd, Michael, *Earthspirit: A Handbook for Nurturing an Ecological Christianity* (Mystic, CT: Twenty-Third Publications, 1991), p. 21.

3. McFague, Sallie, *The Body of God: An Ecological Theology* (Minneapolis: Fortress Press, 1993), pp. 40-42.

4. Swimme, Brian, *The Universe is a Green Dragon* (Santa Fe: Bear & Company, 1984), pp. 58-9, 67.

5. Ibid., p. 170.

6. Edwards, Denis, *Jesus and the Cosmos* (Homebush, New South Wales: St. Paul Publications, 1991), pp. 22-23. (See Bibliography for U.S. ed.)

7. *Encyclopedic World Atlas* (Chicago: Rand McNally, 1990), p. 3.

8. Gribbin, John, *In the Beginning: The Birth of the Living Universe* (London: Penguin Books, 1994), p. xiii.

9. *Encyclopedic World Atlas*, pp. 33-44; cf *The Guiness Encyclopedia* (Middlesex: Guiness Publishing, Ltd., 1990); Gamlin, Linda, *Origins of Life: Today's World Series* (London: Gloucester Press, 1988).

10. Dowd, *Earthspirit*, pp. 23.

11. *Catechism of the Catholic Church* (Collegeville, MN: The Liturgical Press, 1994).

REFLECTION

• What is it in the contemporary understanding of our universe, Earth's place in it, and the development of life on Earth that most surprises and moves me to wonder?

• What is it in this understanding that most challenges or has challenged my images about God?

• What other story (among many) in the Old Testament do I now recognize as myth? What is the religious truth or insight the story conveys?

• Are there Gospel stories I now recognize should be interpreted as myth rather than as literal descriptions of events?

• When did I move from literal understanding to acceptance of a symbolic meaning? Who or what helped me? Has it made the stories richer or diminished their importance?

RECOMMENDED READING

1. Swimme, Brian; *The Universe is a Green Dragon*. This delightful book evokes awe and wonder.

2. Dowd, Michael; *Earthspirit*. Presents facts and challenges in simple language, and has many interesting quotations from various sources.

3. Birch, Charles; *On Purpose*. Not recreational reading, but well worth the effort.

CHAPTER THREE

God in Us

The redemption model has been the most influential, prevailing, and underlying pattern of thought in Christian thinking about God. As we saw in the first two chapters, this understanding of God and our relationship with God was shaped by the thought patterns and the worldview of Jewish and early Christian culture, and suffers from the limitations of an outmoded cosmology.

Today, in another time, another culture, another worldview we need to ensure that our ideas about God are relevant to the contemporary understanding of the universe and our place in it—and also allow for further developments that might change our understanding of our place in the universe.

If we continue to uphold, as the *Catechism* does, the worldview from which redemption theology emerged; if we stay with a literalist, fundamentalist understanding of Scripture; if we have no understanding of the way thought patterns of particular cultures and particular ages shaped and packaged truths and insights, there is little hope for church doctrine to be relevant in today's society. At the same time, a significant number of Christians will simply not budge from what they believe are absolute, final, not-to-be-questioned ways of imaging God, Jesus, church, and ourselves.

When our understanding of our universe with regard to time and distances and our place in it has undergone such extraordinary changes in our lifetime (with much more to come) we find ourselves having to adjust or even radically change some of our ideas about God. One of our main foundational ideas about God, however, remains constant and we can use this as a base from which to explore the religious consequences of new knowledge about ourselves in this universe. This foundation is our traditional Christian belief that God is present to everything that exists, that nothing can have existence without the presence of God sustaining it. One of the biggest challenges facing us is to be thorough and radical in our attempt to describe the implications of this.

God in All Things

Let us begin to face the challenge by starting with the basic truth of incarnation. Traditional Christianity has no problems with the concept that in Jesus God became human. Here is change in God; here is involvement; here is response and movement; here is compassion.

What if we were to take this basic Christian understanding of God's involvement with humanity and push it back to the beginning of creation? What if, still being beyond and greater than the sum total of creation, God was "incarnated" into all of creation, so that all of creation is infused with, sustained by, driven by the energy that is of God?

Immediately, we have to image God differently. We have to let go of the localizing tendency and allow the name "God" to depict, on the one hand, a limitless, infinitely vast reality, totally beyond our imagining. We cannot localize this reality into a "he" who is in heaven. On the other hand, God must be present everywhere as the life-force, or energy, or power—whatever it is that sustains and energizes life. But we must also caution that this is not a definition of what

"God" is. It is simply inadequate language struggling to be in touch with the truth of incarnation—God in all, with all, and through all. We are simply trying to make sense of the reality we name as "God" rather than assert that *this* is what God *is*.

We can assert that everything in existence is permeated with the presence of God. Let us be clear: we are not talking about some shadowy presence like a cloud moving through a forest. No, we are talking about a presence within the depths of all that is. For humans we would point to the love that is in our hearts; we would point to DNA (deoxyribonucleic acid, nucleic acids in chromosomes of higher organisms which store genetic information), and the atoms and molecules in our bodily structure where there is spontaneity and life and movement; where there is growth; where, because there is freedom of movement and limitless possibilities, there is also illness as well as health. This is incarnation at the most basic level. God really is *in* and *with* and *through* all. But we have to adapt our image of God, don't we, if we are to take this seriously?

Yet none of this is news to us. We have always stated that "God is everywhere": we just haven't taken the statement seriously and thought it through. We also haven't had today's knowledge about the universe and the development of life on our planet as the worldview in which to think about it. Modern scientific knowledge can help us appreciate better this incarnational aspect of God's presence.

With reference to the chart on page 27-28 which outlined the development of life on this planet, we can contrast two different ways of thinking about God's creative activity.

In the mechanistic worldview, and often in popular imagination, God is seen as totally distinct from creation, over and above it. God is the Overseer. God orders and arranges as God wishes. Everything is in God's hands, and God plans developments step by step. The mechanistic understanding of physics fitted well with this mechanistic model of God. God could just rearrange or order things as God wished. God was the Great External Designer: that goes with this and this goes with that and the universe is in good hands. God arranged the building blocks and then one day decided to put human beings on the planet. Or God as an outside agent, designed and directed everything to make our existence possible.

Sallie McFague comments on this:

> It is significant that deism—the understanding of God as external to the world, intervening at most only to initiate creation and fill in the gaps in our present knowledge and power—accompanies the machine model. And this is the God that is still all too current in many contemporary church circles: a personal, external superperson who intervenes in the lives of particular individuals at times of stress and despair to fix problems. God is the ultimate Fixer of a malfunctioning world machine....[1]

Another way of thinking about God's creative activity stems from modern scientific thought about the way the universe functions. Central to this is the understanding of "mind." Our tendency is to think of mind only as we experience this in ourselves, i.e., a conscious function. But in scientific understanding, mind is not confined to being a conscious function linked to a brain. Mind is in all matter, and lifeless matter is not as inactive in the core of itself as we have been accustomed to believe. This is a new perspective for many of us. Bede Griffiths provides a helpful summary:

> We have seen that there is an organizing power at every level and this organizing power has the character of a mind. Mind, it has been said, reveals itself as a "pattern of self-organization and a set of dynamic relationships." In this sense it can be said that mind is present in matter from the beginning...mind is present in matter, and in plants and animals, and that mind becomes conscious in us. And so, in a very exact sense, it can be said that matter becomes conscious in human beings....[2]

Modern science is telling us that we cannot continue to separate the material world into lifeless matter and mind as two completely different realities, nor link mind only with what has consciousness. Quantum physics, insists Charles Birch, "forces us to view mind and matter as single aspects of one phenomenon...It is mind-matter."[3]

Mind is present in all things; mind becomes *conscious* in human beings. Here is a scientific model of thinking that allows us to imagine God's presence permeating everything that has existence, and human beings in a special way. And this creative presence—call it Mind or call it Life Energy or any other name—allows for chance and freedom and spontaneity and the totally unexpected.

A scientist specializing in quantum physics will not necessarily associate "mind-matter" with the presence of God. That association belongs to the realm of faith. It is a response to the religious question: if we believe in a God, where and how would we expect to find this reality present? The association is not intended to state that THIS is what God is. Rather, it is intended to suggest how we might be thinking if we took seriously the notion of God being present in and through everything that has existence. Here God is understood as an incarnational presence rather than an external manipulator. God works in and through and with what God has to work with. There is limitation here and adaptability, as well as unimaginable diversity and possibilities.

Wherever the presence of God is one would expect to find variety, spontaneity, change, growth, development, new possibilities, adaptability, and even disorder (the price of freedom and chance encounters). Sallie McFague comments:

> All of us, living and non-living, are one phenomenon, a phenomenon stretching over billions of years and containing untold numbers of strange, diverse, and marvelous forms of matter—including our own. The universe is a body, to use a poor analogy from our own experience, but it is not a human body; rather, it is matter bodied forth seemingly infinitely, diversely, endlessly, yet internally as one.
>
> Is this a model within which to live on planet Earth for the twenty-first century? Is this also a model with which Christians might express the relation of God and the world? Is this a model that will help us to gain an appropriate sense of our place in the

scheme of things as well as reimagine the immanence and transcendence of the Western God?[4]

Michael Dowd notes

...that at no point in time during the past four and a half billion years, the age of our solar system, did anyone come from outside and put anything on the planet. God is the inner dynamic guiding the process, the living reality revealed in and through creation....[5]

CREATED IN GOD'S IMAGE

Human beings as life forms "created in God's image" take on new significance in this perspective. All of creation is permeated with the presence of God. The wonder of human existence is that human beings can be conscious of this presence and give it a name. We can identify ourselves in terms of its reality. From it we can derive significance and give meaning to our lives. We can marvel at who and what we are. We can give praise and thanks on behalf of all of creation; we can allow this faith to shape our lives and the destiny of life on this planet.

Think of the wonder of human existence. We literally give God a voice and arms; we give love shape and form—we embody it. It is literally true that God (as spirit) cannot speak. You need a body to make sounds. God (as spirit) cannot write music. God (as spirit) cannot write poetry. God (as spirit) cannot tell me God loves me, nor can God put God's arms around me and nurture me into wholeness. But the God who comes to human expression in Mozart or Beethoven produces music that will forever touch human lives. The God embodied in Keats or Shelley produces poetry that will forever touch human hearts and minds. My parents and my brothers and sisters tell me they love me and nurture me. Am I not to believe that in them the reality of God is given human form?

A perspective such as this also provides us with the foundations for a spirituality which resonates with and leads to involvement in the environmental issues of today. We can no longer afford to act out of a spirituality that asserted human mastery over the rest of creation and that we could do with the material world whatever we wished. We are not "masters of"; we are one with, nurtured into life by, totally dependent on Earth's life systems.

Much is being written and spoken about this today. One Catholic theologian addressing ecological issues is Thomas Berry. He insists that our world is not simply an "object" at the disposal of humans. It is not ours to manipulate and exploit simply for our gain or profit. He calls our attention to the "maternal" aspect of this world that has nourished us into existence, that the natural world is a sacred place:

> The natural world is the larger sacred community to which we belong. To be alienated from this community is to become destitute in all that makes us human. To damage this community is to diminish our own existence.

> If this sense of the sacred character of the natural world as our primary revelation of the divine is our first need, our second need is to diminish our emphasis on redemption experience in favor of a greater emphasis on creation process....We need to see ourselves as integral with this emergent process, as that being in whom the universe reflects on and celebrates itself. Once we begin to experience ourselves in this manner, we immediately perceive how adverse to our own well-being psychically and spiritually as well as economically is any degradation of the planet.[6]

Another perennial concern for theology is the problem of evil. The "problem" aspect depends very much on the image of God and the worldview in which we operate. The first response to the question, "How can God permit evil?" ought to be, "What is your image of God?" If we are dealing with an external manipulator of events who could have made things perfect but, for some reason we cannot fathom, decided to let bad things happen, then we have a problem. But if our image of God focuses on the presence of God in all things and accepts that God can only work within and through a "free" environment if there is to be ongoing, creative development, then we must also accept that some things will necessarily go wrong:

The ordered universe contains within it much that is disordered and incomplete. Multiple creativity makes some disorder and conflict inevitable. It allows for the possibility of great disorder and evil. In the ecological model evil springs from chance and the freedom that it allows—not from providence. The reason providence does not eliminate chance is because a world without chance is a world without freedom. Every natural entity, every atom must have an aspect of self-determination or spontaneity and the intersection of even two, let alone myriads, acts of self-determination is precisely chance. For God to completely control the world would be the same as to annihilate it. It follows that it is nonsense to ask the question—why did God allow Vesuvius to pour its molten lava on populated Pompeii, or why did God allow the Holocaust? People who ask such questions have not been liberated from the concept of God as omnipotent dictator of the universe, responsible for everything that happens and who, if he willed, could change the course of events by sheer fiat. This concept has infused tragedy into the histories of Christianity and Mohammedanism. When catastrophe strikes people ask—why did God do this to me? It is a non-question because God does not manipulate things and people.[7]

Our religious language, however, sometimes promotes the idea that God *does* manipulate. Language about "God's will" constantly does so. We would do well to explore what our image of God is whenever we find ourselves using this language about God. If, for example, a woman's husband dies suddenly of a heart attack, what image of God is conveyed by telling her it must be what God wanted? Or, what image of God is given to the children of this couple when the priest at the funeral Mass makes a statement to the effect that "God has taken" this man from us?

Wouldn't it be more faithful to what we Christians believe about God to assert that God is fundamentally, absolutely, infinitely, loving and life-giving, but operates within a necessarily free (for the sake of development), imperfect (a necessary result of freedom) universe?

What God "wants," or what God's activity is always directed toward, are life, growth, love, and union.

But accidents happen; things go wrong; people are capable of evil; death is a natural reality in this imperfect, developing world, and the nature of death can, in some circumstances, be surrounded with pain and tragedy. Where is God? Surely, God has to be in it. And surely, God also has to be beyond it. This is the hope and the faith we live by: death is not the end; death is the entrance into the fullness of the mystery of God's life and love.

NOTES

1. McFague, *The Body of God*, p. 37.
2. Griffiths, Bede, *A New Vision of Reality* (London: Fount Paperbacks, 1992), pp 258-263. (See Bibliography for U.S. ed.)
3. Birch, *On Purpose*, p. 75.
4. McFague, op. cit., p. 97.
5. Dowd, *Earthspirit*, p. 18.
6. Berry, Thomas, *The Dream of the Earth* (San Francisco: Sierra Club Books, 1990), p. 82.
7. Birch, op. cit., p. 93-94.

REFLECTION

• Who has embodied, and who now embodies, God's presence for me in a special way? What do I now know about God from knowing these people?

• For whom do I embody God's presence in a special way? What do I imagine people know about God from knowing me?

• In what practical way do I show respect for the environment?

• What are some implications from this chapter for religious language such as "God's will" or "vocation"?

RECOMMENDED READING

1. Griffiths, Bede; *A New Vision of Reality.* Highly recommended.
2. Berry, Thomas; *The Dream of the Earth.*

CHAPTER FOUR

Revelation

The two quite different models of imaging God and the way God is (or is not) present in creation, outlined in the previous chapter, result in two very different models or understandings of

GOD
↓
ISAIAH
🚶
↓
THE HEBREWS

revelation—the way the reality of God is revealed in our world. This in turn influences the way we understand Scripture to be "inspired" by God and can lead us to a new appreciation of how Scripture took shape.

In the traditional model of understanding revelation and inspiration, God "out there" decided to communicate directly with people. God wanted to reveal "himself," so God chose a people (the Hebrews in the Old Testament) and individuals within that group of people through whom to communicate (eg., Moses and Isaiah), as illustrated in this diagram. So the Hebrews understood themselves to be God's chosen people in an exclusive sense. This manner of self-identification was later taken over by the church, and blended well with the redemption model of understanding God's relationship with us. The *Catechism of the Catholic Church* presents this schema:

- God "manifested himself to our first parents from the very beginning..." and "clothed them with resplendent grace and justice" (#54).

- After the fall, "God buoyed them up with the hope of salvation, by promising redemption" (#55).

- "After the unity of the human race was shattered by sin God at once sought to save humanity part by part" (#56).

- God called Abraham. "The people descended from Abraham would be the trustees of the promise made to the patriarchs, the chosen people, called to prepare for that day when God would gather all his children into the unity of the church" (#59).

- "God forms his people Israel in the hope of salvation, in the expectation of a new and everlasting Covenant intended for all" (#64).

- Jesus is the "Father's definitive Word; so there will be no further Revelation after him" (#73).

Note how, in #59, there is still an expectation that God will gather all people into the "unity of the Church." This highlights one of the central weaknesses of the model and it is found in other religions as well. This is the claim to exclusivity, the claim to be the ONE authentic bearer of the divine presence in the world, the ONE authentic voice of the divine presence and with it the expectation that all the world has to be converted to it as the ONE authentic religion.

This sense of exclusiveness within religious movements often went hand in hand with an experience of being a small group, constantly under threat and conscious of an important destiny:

The more threatened this elect people felt, the more intensely they experienced their own significance as a people destined to be the instrument of divine rule over all the nations of the world.[1]

Another major weakness in the model is the way its understanding of divine inspiration and revelation leads to fundamentalist and literalist approaches to Scripture, i.e., approaches which understand "the inspired Word of God" almost as dictation from heaven. In that case, everything recorded in Scripture must be literally true and there cannot be errors of any kind. Late last century and for most of this century Catholic Scripture scholars have had to battle against suspicion and criticism within the church because they questioned fundamentalist or literalist approaches to Scripture. The eminent Catholic Scripture scholar, Raymond Brown, wrote in 1975,

> The battle of biblical criticism has been to get Christians and the church to recognize that the books of the Bible contain the word of God phrased in the words of men and that therefore to discover God's revelation one must take into account the historical situation, the philosophical worldview, and the theological limitations of the men who wrote them. The same battle has to be won in relation to the dogmas of the church where once again God's revelation has been phrased by men.[2]

Brown is reflecting here a more contemporary view of revelation that avoids the two major weaknesses mentioned above. Here, Scripture is not understood as dictation from heaven. God does not operate as an outsider, distant from us. In fact, God cannot be elsewhere and not here at the same time. God can never be absent. God present works with what God has to work with. If, then, we are to understand and appreciate the Hebrew and Christian Scriptures, we need to understand and appreciate the cultures, worldviews, time, place, ways of communicating, literary style, thought patterns, and community or historical circumstances in which they took shape. These are what God has to work with. These inevitably give shape to the ways God's presence is experienced and described.

In recent years, the Pontifical Biblical Commission has issued documents helping Catholics to appreciate this understanding of revelation and to move beyond fundamentalist approaches to Scripture. In one document we read:

The basic problem with fundamentalist interpretation…is that, refusing to take into account the historical character of biblical revelation, it makes itself incapable of accepting the full truth of the Incarnation itself.…It refuses to admit that the inspired Word of God has been expressed in human language and that this Word has been expressed under divine inspiration, by human authors possessed of limited capacities and resources. For this reason, it tends to treat the biblical text as if it had been dictated word for word by the Spirit. It fails to recognize that the Word of God has been formulated in language and expression conditioned by various periods.…

Fundamentalism likewise tends to adopt very narrow points of view. It accepts the literal reality of an ancient, out-of-date cosmology, simply because it is expressed in the Bible…[3]

If we take guidance from the teaching of the Pontifical Biblical Commission and apply it, for example, to our understanding of the prophet Isaiah in Hebrew Scripture, we appreciate that the Spirit of God at work in a particular culture, place, time, and worldview came to expression in a particular person who then preached "the word of God." This is how inspiration by God's Spirit works.

We can take this insight into the nature of God's revelation a step further. If God is truly always present everywhere, we should expect God's presence and something of God's nature to be revealed in all of creation. We should expect and take seriously that God's presence, God's spirit, has been and is at work in all people, in all places, at all times, in a multitude of differing cultures, thought patterns, and worldviews. God's presence and insights into the nature of God will surface differently within those human factors. In a very real way, different cultures shape their understanding of God. This is inevitable. It is as true for the Jewish culture as it is for the Buddhist culture.

This is a challenge to any exclusive claims to God's revelation. If we image God as all pervasive, in and through all that exists, we must believe in God's Spirit actively working in all cultures, in all places, at all times, within greatly divergent thought patterns and worldviews.

THE INCLUSIVENESS OF GOD

We know that in the thousand years before Jesus was born there was an enormous surge in religious thinking across the world:

> Apparently quite independently, spiritual leaders arose across the world in the sixth century BC. There lived then in China, Confucius and Lao-tzu, in India, Gautama Buddha, and in Persia, Zoroaster. Thales and Pythagoras were founding Greek philosophy and the prophetic movement in Israel had reached a climax in second-Isaiah.[4]

We have to consider *and accept* that the same Spirit of God which was active in Israel was active all over the world, necessarily working within and bound to varying cultures, places, worldviews, thought patterns, and individuals. This knowledge presents us with a radically different view of revelation. Here we are challenged to take seriously not only the reality that God is at work in all cultures, but that the images of and ideas about God which emerge are necessarily produced by and tied to that particular culture.

God works with what God has to work with. This is incarnation in its most radical understanding. Within this framework we must continue to assert that God is beyond our culturally defined images and ideas. We can never claim that we are actually imaging or describing what or who "God" is.

This viewpoint challenges the *exclusive* claims of any particular religion which wants to emphasize that "We are the *only true* religion. We alone have God's revelation. We have God on our side; you don't." Or, "If you want to be 'saved' you have to accept our culture, our thought patterns, our dogmas, and our rituals, otherwise there is no hope for you."

The tendency of human beings to lock God's revelation into their own culture and thought patterns in an exclusive fashion is remarkable! The history of religions is plagued with wars, the decimation of cultures, the inability to recognize God's presence in different cultures, and the refusal to accept that another religious tradition might have insights into the transcendent which might enrich one's own religious understandings. Only now are we changing, albeit very slowly, and beginning to appreciate that God's presence and activity in our world are not locked into any one religious movement. We need to understand both the universality of God's presence as well as the way it has been and always will be embodied in particular cultures and thought patterns. Bede Griffith comments:

> All the great revelations are, as it were, messages from that transcendent world. They are given in the Scriptures of the various great traditions, the Vedas and Upanishads, the Quran, the Buddhist Scriptures, and the Bible. They are all revelations of transcendent reality. Then again the process is that the revelations are interpreted by the rational mind and so there are the great theologians and philosophers, for example, Sankara and Ramanuja for Hinduism; Nagarjuna, Asanga, and Vasubandhu for Buddhism; Ibn al Arabi and al Ghazzali for Islam; St. Thomas Aquinas, St. Bonaventure, and others for Christianity.
>
> These great thinkers bring the rational mind to bear on the transcendent mysteries which are realities of experience. It is important to realize this because so often the impression is given these revelations are, as it were, dropped from heaven, and people tend to accept them uncritically and therefore to misunderstand them. The reality is that all religious truth comes from an original experience, that of the seer, the prophet, the saint. But the experience always has to be interpreted in the light of rational, conceptual thought.[5]

If we accept the basic premise that God is at work in all places, at all times, in all people—and we must do so—then we Christians will have to change our understanding of "revelation" as we have been accustomed to think of it. Revelation is not a matter of an external deity trying to break into human affairs through the medium of a particular group. We have to look in all religious groups for signs of God's presence and for insights to understanding the nature of God. As Christians, we will still hold to the insights and understandings that have been and are "Christian"; we will still have Jesus central to our belief system; we will still need the community we name "church." But in sharing our insights and understandings we will no longer see ourselves as the only door to the sacred, and will be open to learning from other religious systems of belief.

This broader understanding of revelation which gives due recognition to God's Spirit working everywhere, challenges the Christian churches and other religious systems to move beyond their own boundaries. While never losing their own unique identities and charisms they must collectively try to harness for the good of humankind the beliefs they share in the reality of God. Are there stories and symbols and realities that can be common ground for the major religions of the world? Is there a way of understanding revelation that could bring people of different religious persuasions together rather than driving them apart and accentuating differences? Brian Swimme comments:

> For the first time in human history, we have in common an origin story of the universe that already captivates minds on every continent of our planet. No matter what racial, religious, cultural, or national background, humans now have a unifying language out of which we can begin to organize ourselves, for the first time, on the level of species.[6]

Modern cosmology offers the major religions of the world the chance to dialogue and share insights about the sacred. It offers a common story with which to dialogue. It offers the opportunity to move from stances of exclusivity, suspicion, and status. Thomas Berry believes today's scientific understanding of the birth and development of our universe is a key to fruitful religious dialogue:

> We need a new type of religious orientation. This must, in my view, emerge from our new story of the universe....
>
> We must begin where everything begins in human affairs—with the basic story, our narrative of how things came to be, how they came to be as they are, and how the future can give us some satisfying direction. We need a story that will educate us, a story that will heal, guide, and discipline us.[7]

The challenges are obviously enormous. Each religion, while affirming its own distinctive religious message, has to deal with any fundamentalist and exclusive stances if dialogue is to bear fruit. In particular, issues bearing on images of God, the nature of revelation, and how religions depict themselves as authoritative bearers of that revelation will be central.

Clearly, for Christians, the mechanistic, manipulating deity who intervenes from outside and deigns to speak to us from a great height has had its day as a worthwhile image of God. God's is not a voice breaking through from outer space into our world. While we believe that in speaking of God we are speaking of an infinite reality over and beyond the material universe, we want to affirm also that the primary arena in which this infinite being is revealed to us is *in* the world in which we live. This is as true today as it was two thousand years ago when people came to believe they experienced the divine presence in a human person, Jesus.

NOTES

1. Berry, Thomas, "The Earth: A New Context for Religious Unity" in Lonergan, Anne & Richards, Caroline, eds., *Thomas Berry and the New Cosmology* (Mystic: CT: Twenty-Third Publications, 1987), pp. 29-30.

2. Brown, Raymond, *Biblical Reflections on Crises Facing the Church* (London: Darton, Longman & Todd, 1975), p. 116. (See Bibliography for U.S. ed.)

3. Pontifical Biblical Commission, *The Interpretation of the Bible in the Church* (Boston: Pauline Books & Media, 1993), pp. 73-74.

4. Birch, *On Purpose*, p. 107.

5. Griffith, *A New Vision of Reality*, pp. 267-268.

6. Swimme, *The Universe is a Green Dragon*, p. 161.

7. Berry, *The Dream of the Earth*, p. 87; 124.

REFLECTION

• How have I been accustomed to understanding revelation? Who or what were major influences in that understanding?

• What do I think are significant challenges to Christianity in general and the Catholic Church in particular from a broader understanding of revelation?

• In what ways have I experienced or noticed God's revelation in non-Christian religious groups?

- In what events of my life do I recognize God's revelation?
- Why is Jesus considered by Christians to be unique in the unfolding of God's revelation on Earth?

RECOMMENDED READING

Capra, Fritjof and David Steindl-Rast, with Thomas Matus; *Belonging to the Universe: New Thinking About God and Nature.* London: Penguin Books, 1992.

CHAPTER FIVE

Understanding Jesus

In general Christian thinking, Jesus is understood as the incarnation, the taking flesh, of the Second Person of the Blessed Trinity—sent down from heaven by the Father to redress the wrong human beings had done and to win back God's friendship. Jesus' role was to "save" us by effecting a change of attitude in God, who then opened the gates of heaven. The divine nature of Jesus is heavily stressed because the bottom line is that if Jesus is not divine we are not saved, for we as mere human beings are incapable of redressing the wrong done to God by the sin of our first parents. Concepts such as "salvation" and "redemption" have usually been understood within this framework.

This viewpoint, as we will see, also takes for granted that Jesus knew precisely who he was (God become human), how unique he was, and what his role was.

Anyone questioning this conventional understanding about Jesus runs the risk of being declared a heretic. Indeed, it comes as quite a shock to many Christians that this way of understanding Jesus and his role could be questioned at all.

Yet it is being questioned, and will continue to be questioned because its critics believe this way of thinking is founded on a religious worldview that is no longer relevant as an explanation of God's relationship with human beings. It is founded on an outdated cosmology which presumes God is up or out there somewhere and sends his Son down to this planet. That cosmology does not take seriously the reality that the whole universe is permeated with the presence of God; it presumes the sacred, the divine is basically elsewhere and visits us, or deigns to break into our exiled world in unusual ways.

The task in this chapter is to explore how Jesus came to be understood in conventional Christian thinking and to examine some of the questions being raised today concerning the way Jesus' role in human affairs has been interpreted.

Our starting point is the Gospels.

It is enormously important for Christians to understand how and when the Gospels were formed and how this influenced *what* was written. Without an informed understanding of the formation of the Gospels, fundamentalist and literalist approaches will continue to distort the original meanings of the text. How the Gospels came to life and how the Christian community wrestled with the questions about Jesus' identity will hopefully provide a basis for understanding why many scholars today are questioning traditional language about salvation and Jesus as savior.

Most Catholics do not know that the Gospels were written many years after Jesus' death. The common understanding is that they were eyewitness accounts, written soon after the resurrection, or even during his lifetime. Catholics would also generally believe that Jesus spoke every word attributed to him and that every event in the Gospels happened as recorded. This was certainly *not* the case.

Some of the critical points to understand and appreciate about the formation of the Gospels include the following:

• The Gospels were written well after the resurrection, and the resurrection was like a filter through which the writers looked back on Jesus' life—and colored it accordingly.

• The letters of St. Paul appeared before the Gospels.

• A strong oral tradition existed in the Christian communities for about 40 years before the Gospels were written.

• Particular early Christian communities produced the Gospels. Life and events in these communities shaped some of the content and particular emphasis of each Gospel.

• Mark is the first Gospel; it did not appear until about 40 years after Jesus' death.

• The Gospels of Matthew and Luke, while copying much of Mark, include other material about Jesus. Some of this additional material is from a source common to both. Some of it is unique to each of them.

• Apart from Luke, the Gospels are the final work of editors. Matthew's Gospel was not penned by the apostle Matthew. He would have been dead before the Gospel came into existence. Mark and Luke were not apostles. St. John also would have been long dead before the Gospel which bears his name appeared.

• The infancy accounts in Matthew and Luke were not written as historical biography. They were written, in the light of the resurrection, to tell WHO this child is for us. The stories are symbolic and they provided a truth the early Christians were willing to die for: Jesus IS savior. The stories belong to a type of literature that was common to the oral and literary tradition of the time: tracing the origin of a great prophet back to his birth.[1]

• The Annunciation needs to be appreciated not as an actual event, but as later understanding of Jesus put into an "annunciation" format, as happened with other famous people: Isaac (Gn 17), Moses (Ex 3), Gideon (Jgs 6), Samson (Jgs 13), and John the Baptist (Lk 1). This is a literary device or format whereby after the death of a famous person his deeds are "foretold" in stories about his birth or about how God chose this person for a particular role.

• John's Gospel was a long time in the making and is not a word-for-word account by John the apostle. Much of this Gospel is theological reflection about Jesus in the light of the resurrection. The Jesus who walked this Earth certainly did not utter the long discourses found in John's Gospel. Nor is it likely that Jesus recited chapters 13-17 of John's Gospel at the Last Supper.

The Gospel is "inspired" by the Spirit working in the minds of brilliant people who reflected on the meaning of Jesus and his place in the life of the Christian community. The people who finally edited John's Gospel (very late in the first century) had no hesitation about weaving their post-resurrection theological understanding of Jesus into the Gospel, for example, in the Prologue and Jesus' discourses. For the writers and editors of this Gospel the point of the discourses is not whether Jesus actually uttered these words, but rather, do these words reflect the truth of who Jesus is for us? More importantly: would we be willing to die for the truth (a strong theme in the Gospel) expressed in these passages?

Many of us undoubtedly find some of these points disturbing when we first hear them. We clearly need help and guidance if some of our strongly held beliefs about the Gospels are being challenged.

The Pontifical Biblical Commission has tried over the years to give guidance in the monumental task of educating us to a better understanding of the formation of the Gospels. The Commission's 1984 document provided this summary:

> The gospel traditions were gathered and gradually committed to writing in the light of Easter, until at length they took a fixed form in four booklets. These booklets do not simply contain things "that Jesus began to do and to teach" (Acts 1:1); they also present theological interpretations of such things....In these booklets, then, one must learn to look for the Christology of each evangelist. This is especially true of John, who in the patristic period would receive the title, "Theologian." Similarly, other authors whose writings are preserved in the New Testament have interpreted the deeds and sayings of Jesus in diverse ways, and even more so his death and resurrection.[2]

A more recent document from the Commission warns of the dangers of not taking into account the "development of the gospel tradition" and "naively confusing" what finally came to be written in the

Gospels with the initial words and deeds of Jesus. The section on fundamentalism in the 1993 document includes this statement:

> In what concerns the Gospels, fundamentalism does not take into account the development of the gospel tradition, but naively confuses the final stage of this tradition (what the evangelists have written) with the initial (the words and deeds of the historical Jesus).[3]

It is important for us to realize there are "theological interpretations" in the Gospels, that each editor shaped material to present Jesus in a particular light, and that John's Gospel especially contains much post-resurrection theological reflection on Jesus, some of which is simply put onto Jesus' lips. It is equally important for the various Christian churches to help their believers to become familiar with and accepting of contemporary scriptural scholarship. John Hick mentions the reactions of some Christians, who are

> ...indignant that the churches had so long encouraged them to go on innocently assuming, for example, that the historical Jesus had said, "I and the Father are one" (Jn 10:30), "He who has seen me has seen the Father" (Jn 14:9), rather than revealing the scholarly consensus that a writer some sixty or more years later, expressing the theology that had developed in his part of the church, put these famous words into Jesus' mouth. Indeed these Christians were indignant that the churches so generally failed to treat them as intelligent adults who could be trusted with the results of biblical and theological scholarship.[4]

The point is that the Gospels were written to express what the Christian communities came to believe about Jesus in the light of the resurrection rather than being biographies. Without this realization, the Gospels will continue to be quoted in a literalist fashion in an effort to "prove" that Jesus knew all along he was the Son of God, the Second Person of the Trinity. This manner of quoting the Gospels, especially John's Gospel, sometimes prevents people from entering into serious consideration of the totally human reality of Jesus.

DEVELOPMENT OF THE GOSPEL NARRATIVE

Scholarship today is prompting us to keep two factors clearly in mind in our approach to the Gospels. The first is that the post-resurrection understanding of Jesus' divinity is written into the Gospels as if that understanding were there in his lifetime. We need to know it was not there in his lifetime. Our understanding of this fact will influence, for example, whether we believe Mary knew from the moment of conception or at the birth of Jesus that he was God, or whether we doubt that Mary, being a Jewish woman, could ever have considered such a possibility. Taking the infancy stories as factual accounts makes it difficult for us to come to terms with a different appreciation of how Mary may have had many questions, as both a young and an elderly mother, about her son.

The second factor is that the trinitarian language we use today about Jesus and his relationship with God took centuries to evolve. Appreciating this fact will influence whether or not we believe Jesus thought of himself as the incarnation of the Second Person of the Trinity.

Scholarship today traces a development that begins with the Pentecost preaching about a man, a human person like us, through whom God worked wonders, whom God raised. Raised by God, not by his own power, this human person, Jesus, received the fullness of the promised Spirit of God. This quote is from Peter's speech at Pentecost:

> This Jesus God raised up, and of that all of us are witnesses. Being therefore exalted at the right hand of God, and having received from the Father the promise of the Holy Spirit, he has poured out this that you both see and hear (Acts 2:32–33).

Clearly, this passage does not identify Jesus with or as God. It is in recognition of his resurrection that titles of exaltation were given to Jesus. Only after the resurrection was he understood as the anointed one, "Christ," "Lord," and "Son of God." However, it needs to be noted that the title "son of God" did not have the connotations of identification with God that developed later in trinitarian thought. Paul says that

"Everyone moved by the Spirit is a son of God" (Rom 8:14).

"Son of God" was not an exceptional title at the time of Jesus. It was a term widely used for the Roman ruler, Augustus. It was a common term in Greek mythology and Egyptian rulers were called sons of God. The Dead Sea scrolls refer to the "son of the Great God." James Dunn comments that in all likelihood Jesus used the title of himself, but not in the sense it later came to mean. Rather, it was in the sense that he prayed to God as "Father." Dunn concludes that at the time of Jesus "son of God" was generally used of a person who was thought "to be commissioned by God or highly favored by God."[5]

John Hick comments that it is neither surprising nor remarkable "that Jesus should have come to be regarded as belonging to the class of divine persons." There was a "widespread honorific divinizing of outstanding religious figures" and Jesus' fame as a preacher, prophet, and healer would have been enough for him to earn the "son of God" accolade.[6]

The next stage in the development of Christian understanding about Jesus was the use of titles of exaltation (following from the resurrection) to speak about Jesus in his lifetime. Biblical scholars have a name for this: "retrojection."[7] When the Gospels came to be formed, the writers and editors put back into Jesus' lifetime, and onto his lips, titles which initially were only used to speak of the post-resurrection Jesus. The infancy account in Luke provides an example of this. At the Annunciation, Mary is told,

> You will conceive in your womb and bear a son, and you will name him Jesus. He will be great, and will be called the Son of the Most High....Therefore the child to be born will be holy; he will be called Son of God (Lk 1:31–35).

This text is often quoted by people to "prove" that even before Jesus was born, Mary knew he was God. It takes much patient work to convince people the text cannot be quoted for this purpose, that it is, in fact, an instance of retrojection.

The identification of Jesus with/as God took time to develop. Certainly, there is no trinitarian theology (as later understood in

Greek and traditional Christian thought) in the Gospels, even if some words in John, e.g., "I am in the Father and the Father is in me." (14:10), suggests there is. For Jesus also says, "the Father is greater than I" (14:28), and "Father, may they be one in us, as you are in me and I am in you" (17:21). In this last quote the meaning is surely that whatever union Jesus shares with the "Father" we too share it.

Hans Küng points out that although there are many "triadic formulas" (referring to Father, Son, and Spirit) in the New Testament, "there is not a word anywhere in the New Testament about the unity of these three highly different entities, a unity on the same divine level."[8] It would have been unthinkable for the early Jewish-Christians to identify even the exalted post-resurrection Jesus with God. Jesus stands at the right side of the throne of God, in glory, in total communion with God, "as a human being, the human representative before God."[9]

We need to be clear that scholars are not trying to undermine the reality of Jesus' divinity. Their point is that the trinitarian understanding of divinity as three persons "one in being with" each other and the identification of Jesus with such an understanding, came after the New Testament was written and should not be read into statements about the Father, Son, and Spirit in the New Testament. Raymond Brown comments,

> It would be difficult to find serious contemporary support for the thesis that Jesus used of himself or accepted the "higher" titles of later NT Christology, e.g., "Lord" in the full sense, "Son of God" or "God." (This does not mean that scholars who deny Jesus' use of these titles are saying that Jesus was not Lord, Son of God, or God; it may mean that they regard the application of such designations to have been the result of later Christian reflection on the mystery of Jesus.)[10]

Christianity did not begin with the belief that Jesus was identified with God in the way later trinitarian thought would come to understand him. In its beginnings the Christian movement did not see itself as separate from Judaism. This is significant for Judaism could not in any way accept the idea of a human person being identified with God. What we find in early liturgical texts and in the writings of Paul is the formula: to God (the Father) through, or in the name of Jesus (the human mediator, now at God's side), with the Holy Spirit.

Most New Testament texts used to support later trinitarian doctrine were originally liturgical and creedal texts and fragments. God is called "Father of our Lord Jesus Christ," and the opening greetings in Paul and Deutero-Paul indicate that praise is to be rendered to God through Christ (e.g., Eph 5:20: Give thanks "in the name of our Lord Jesus Christ to God the Father").[11]

In the New Testament, God is always the "God" of Jesus. Jesus prays to God and gives thanks to God. God works through Jesus. It is God who raises Jesus. Even in the text in Philippians where words normally reserved for God are bestowed on Jesus—that at his name every knee should bend in the heavens, on the Earth and under the Earth, and every tongue proclaim that "Jesus Christ is Lord!" (2:11)— it is stressed this is because "God also exalted him" (2:10) and that this is "to the glory of God the Father" (2:11). The exalted and risen Jesus, Jesus as "Lord," still has God as his God.

Another consideration is the early Christian emphasis that what God had worked through Jesus, God would continue to work through the followers of Jesus. Did they not share the same spirit that moved in Jesus? We need to keep our focus on the human dimension here: God did marvelous deeds in and through this human person, Jesus. God has now raised this human person to the fullness of life with God. So with us: God wants to work in us, and we, too, will be raised, just like Jesus. We are, all of us, sons (and daughters) of God:

Do you not know that you are God's temple and that God's Spirit dwells in you (1 Cor 3:16)?

If the Spirit of him who raised Jesus from the dead dwells in you, he who raised Christ from the dead will give life to your mortal bodies also through his Spirit that dwells in you (Rom 8:11).

For all who are led by the Spirit of God are children of God

(Rom 8:14).

We believe...because we know that the one who raised the Lord Jesus will raise us also with Jesus, and will bring us with you into his presence (2 Cor 4:14).

It is also important to note the emphasis in New Testament writings on Jesus not as God, but as the *mediator* between God and ourselves. Christians were urged to pray to the Father or thank the Father "through" Jesus Christ (cf. Rom 1:8; Col 3:17).

From its roots in Judaism, Christianity found in the theme of God's Wisdom another remarkably apt way to speak about Jesus. The Old Testament literature spoke of "Wisdom" being with God, knowing God's works, "present when God made the world" (Wis 9:9). The first chapter of John's Gospel describes Jesus as "the Word" who was with God. That Word, writes John, came into the world, to his own home, and he was not received. The Word became flesh and dwelt (literally, "pitched his tent") among us, says John's Gospel in the Prologue. Sirach 24:8 has Wisdom being instructed by God to "set your tent" (make your dwelling) in Jacob.

Has the writer of John's Gospel identified Jesus with God? We are generally accustomed to think so because of the traditional notion that Jesus, as the Son of God, preexisted with God and came down from heaven to live among us. James Dunn contends that this interpretation cannot be drawn from this text, maintaining that the author of John's Gospel had no intention of identifying Jesus with God. Jesus is the incarnation, the embodiment of that Wisdom which was always with God. Jesus was not always with God.

Again we have deeply entrenched thought patterns based on the way we have "heard" the first words of John's Gospel: "In the beginning was the Word, and the Word was with God." There you are, we say, Jesus is the Word, isn't he?

Dunn maintains translating the first verse of John's Gospel in the sense, "before anything else existed, there was Christ with God" is a serious error, "simply an inadmissible translation." He asserts that for John, Christ is *not* the Word (*logos*, in Greek) but the *Word incarnate.*

In other words, Jesus is the embodiment of the Word (or Wisdom) of God. He is not to be identified with or as the Word or Wisdom. That would be to make the mistake

> ...of identifying Christ as the Logos [Word] even before the incarnation. But in John's christology, Christ, properly speaking, is not the Logos so much as the Logos incarnate. Whereas to speak of Christ as "in the beginning with God" is to imply that the Logos was a quite separate personality from God, a person in the sense that Jesus of Nazareth was a person, already distinct in that sense from God.[12]

This may be heavy reading for 99.9 percent of baptized Christians, but its implications for Christian thinking are enormous, for we are so accustomed to thinking of Jesus as the Christ who preexisted in heaven (that is, someplace else) and came down to Earth. This thinking obviously fits with the trinitarian theology which developed well after Jesus' lifetime. In this theology, the statement that Jesus is divine is linked with him being the Second Person of the Blessed Trinity. Jesus is divine; we are not. Jesus is God; we are not. It is a theology which constantly underlines the belief that Jesus is radically different from us. But if the divinity of Jesus is understood in the sense of a human person who embodies the Wisdom of God and gives witness to that divine Wisdom in the way he lived, then Jesus can be thoroughly human like us and still be divine.

Dunn maintains that Christian thinking shifted from the Wisdom-incarnated-in-Jesus perspective to an emphasis on language about Jesus as the Son of God because such language was more relational. This, in turn, influenced the development of the trinitarian model for thinking about God, when "Son of God" came to imply identification with God.

If Dunn is right, Christianity may need to rethink the necessity of using the trinitarian model as the *only* valid Christian model for interpreting Jesus' relationship with God. It could recover in its common heritage with Judaism another quite different but valid interpretation that blends wonderfully with contemporary cosmology: the reality of the Wisdom or Spirit of God at work in all of creation and coming to unique expression in human beings, created in God's own image. As we shall see, this recovered, radical, interpretation has much to offer Christian spirituality and the ecumenical movement. Divinity is a reality in which we all share.

INFLUENCES ON EARLY THEOLOGY

How and why, then, did Christianity move from an emphasis on Jesus, human like us, the incarnation of God's Wisdom, raised to God's side, mediator, image of our own destiny—all within the framework of Jewish belief in the One God, who was the God of Jesus as well—to Jesus "one in being with," really and truly God, and therefore fundamentally different from us?

How and why did Christianity move from its Jewish roots into arguments about Jesus as God the Son being "consubstantial" with God the Father and God the Holy Spirit, about three persons in one God and about two natures in the person of Jesus? Catherine LaCugna comments on Gregory of Nyssa writing in the fourth century that he could not go to the marketplace to buy bread without getting into a discussion "about whether 'God the Son' is subordinate to 'God the Father,' begotten or unbegotten, created *ex nihilo* or an ordinary man."[13] We are a long way removed from the initial Christian thinking about Jesus here. It is a model of thinking about God that Jesus, as a Jew, would never have dreamed of, and most likely, because he was Jewish, would not have given credence to.

Christian reflection on and understanding of Jesus developed, as would be expected, within the religious worldview and thought patterns of the time and the cultures in which Christianity spread. Both the religious worldview (Jewish and Christian) and the thought patterns (Greek) had an enormous impact on the way Jesus' role was interpreted and then defined as doctrine to be believed.

There were significant factors in the religious worldview of the time which shaped Christian thinking and demanded resolution. Gnosticism was a widespread movement and had such influence in

Christian circles that it became a thorn in the side of Christian leaders. It takes its name from the Greek word *gnosis*, meaning "knowledge." At a time when the established view of a well-ordered universe was breaking down, the gnostics claimed to have special knowledge of and insights into the divine. Within Christianity the gnostics wrote their own scriptures, including gospels, trusted their own religious experiences and knowledge, and generally resisted any claims by church authority regarding "true" teaching. Their worldview was quite complex: matter was evil and God was distant, removed. They selected from Christian thought what suited their own ideas about the way reality connected with the divine. In particular, within Christianity some strands of gnosticism found common ground with speculation that was grounded in Jewish thought: speculation about Adam and Eve; the role of heavenly Wisdom coming to enlighten humans lost in darkness; and the development of baptismal rituals as a way of incorporating human beings into a new, heavenly race free of the constraints of this world.[14]

Gnostic speculation about God and the nature of the world differed from usual Christian thinking. The gnostics' claim to special knowledge and their resistance to church authority with regard to "true" Christian teaching made discussion, debate, and the formulation of clear "orthodox" Christian teaching about God, Jesus as the Redeemer, and God's relationship with the world essential. Walter Kasper, German bishop and theologian, says, "The first phase in the development of the doctrine of the Trinity occurred in the conflict with gnosticism."[15]

The Adam and Eve story played a central role in this development. It meant Jesus was interpreted in the context of a fallen-race-needing-to-be-saved model. As we have already seen, this worldview highlighted the fact that we human beings could not possibly save ourselves and gain entry into heaven. The reasoning was that we human beings are not able to make up to God for the sin of our first parents; only someone from God's side, as it were, could do this. Jesus has saved us, so Jesus must be far more than merely human.

But if he is more than human, if he is really, actually God become human, how could that fit with the traditional truth that God is One? How could Jesus be both human AND God? And the gnostics, with their insistence on the separation of the divine from the depraved material world, argued strongly against the concept of Jesus as both human and divine.

Connected with this understanding of salvation was the issue of Jesus winning for all of us a share in God's life. The connection was: if Jesus is not really God, how can he win for us or offer us a share in God's life? If Christ is not divine (understood now as equal with God), stated orthodox Christian thinking through St. Athanasius, he can neither save us nor make us like God. "God became human, that we might become God," he wrote. And St. Irenaeus, another great scholar defending the need for the trinitarian understanding of God, wrote, "Because of his immeasurable love God became what we are that he might fit us to be what he is."[16]

The issues then became clear and demanded resolution: is Jesus really God? Is he equal to God (the "Father")? If he is really God, how could he be human at the same time? Did Jesus always exist as God before being born on Earth? What of the Scripture references which seem to indicate that Jesus is mediator rather than God, and clearly indicate his belief that "the Father is greater than I" (Jn 14:28)?

Great minds—and they were great minds—wrestled with these questions and strove to formulate answers, answers which ultimately placed an enormous emphasis on the divinity of Jesus, divinity being equated with God. This inevitably set Jesus apart from us, for we are merely human, members of a fallen race. He came to be understood as radically different from us—because he was God. The emphasis on Jesus' divinity and the complex questions it raised overshadowed the human reality of Jesus. Consequently, we have inherited a long tradition of suspicion about speaking of Jesus as human like us (e.g., that his knowledge was limited; he did not know everything).

This theological understanding of Jesus developed very much according to Greek thought patterns. From Greek thought the early church theologians developed an understanding of Jesus as the preexistent Word who had been with God and who came down into our world. (Let us be attuned to the cosmology/worldview operating here, especially the assumption that God is essentially elsewhere and comes from elsewhere to spend time with us.) From Greek thought there developed the understanding of two natures united in one person. And from Greek thought developed a solution to the most vexing theological question about Jesus—his basic relationship with the One God of the Jewish religion. So the doctrine of the Trinity developed.

The Christian church, however, became irrevocably divided on the understanding of what was meant (in Greek) by the term "One in being with" or "consubstantial" with the Father, and on the understanding of two natures in the person of Jesus. Argument was heated, bitterly disputed, and finely focused on the precise meanings of obscure Greek words with which theologians attempted to define orthodox or acceptable Christian thought about Jesus and his relationship with God. The Council of Chalcedon defined what Christians must believe, but at a conservative estimate, 99.99 percent of Christians in the centuries since would have had, and now have, no understanding of the words used to define one of the most important doctrines in Christian history. John Macquarrie comments:

> There are three more or less technical terms that are important in the Chalcedonian definition and that offer a stumbling block to the modern mind: *ousia, hypostasis,* and *physis.* The trouble with these terms is not only that they have their home in an outmoded scheme of philosophy, but that even when they were current, they were ambiguous. Their meanings overlapped, and a glance at a good Greek lexicon will show that the three terms could in different contexts and usages have three distinct meanings, or sometimes they could all flow together in a gloomy semantic merging![17]

Within a few centuries of its beginning the really important issue in Christianity had become right thinking and correct theological terminology. It is easy to dismiss this as an abstract intellectual distraction (because ultimately we know we cannot define in human terms who or what God is), but that would be to miss the underlying concern: how to defend the truth that we are saved and really do have a share in God's life.

Various councils of bishops were held in these early centuries, most notably at Nicaea (325 AD), Constantinople (381 AD), Ephesus (431 AD) and Chalcedon (451 AD). It was, in the words of one historian, "an era of unparalleled importance in the formation of Christian theology." He adds:

> At the same time it was an age of interference and even domination by the emperors, of colorful and abrasive personalities, and of bitter antagonism between leading bishoprics. Technical terms without biblical origins were made key-words in authoritative statements of belief. Their use led to the Latin-speaking West and the Greek-speaking East misunderstanding and misrepresenting one another. Even between different segments of the Greek church misunderstandings arose; these disputes contributed to major divisions in the Christian world.
>
> In theory the first appeal was to Scripture, but the Bible was used in curious or questionable ways. People frequently appealed to Scripture to confirm their theology rather than to decide it. Above all, the disputes were shot through with the feeling that unless God and Christ were truly what Christian devotion and worship proclaimed, then salvation itself was endangered.[18]

From these councils came the formulation of the Christian Creed and centuries of rigorous suppression of any thinking to the contrary. Doctrines about Jesus, developed within the context of a particular time and culture, a literalist understanding of the Fall, a religious worldview that understood God to be distant from us, and the necessity for Jesus to be a God-figure if we are really saved came to be regarded as unchangeable.

Today, there is questioning of both the religious worldview and the thought patterns in which the developing church cemented its understanding of Jesus. There is also questioning of the way the Catholic Church, even today in its official teaching, continues to read back

into the life of Jesus theological ideas which only developed well after
he died.

In the *Catechism*'s treatment of Jesus and his role we find:

No man, not even the holiest, was ever able to take on himself
the sins of all men and offer himself as a sacrifice for all. The
existence in Christ of the divine person of the Son, who at once
surpasses and embraces all human persons and constitutes himself as the Head of all mankind, makes possible his redemptive
sacrifice for all (#616).

The Council of Trent emphasizes the unique character of
Christ's sacrifice as "the source of eternal salvation" and teaches
that "his most holy Passion on the wood of the cross merited
justification for us" (#617).

The *Catechism*, starting with this traditional premise in Christian
redemption theology—that only Jesus as the "divine person of the
Son" is capable of saving us—then deals with the question of Jesus'
self-understanding, and presents these statements:

By its union to the divine wisdom in the person of the Word
incarnate, Christ enjoyed in his human knowledge the fullness of
understanding of the eternal plans he had come to reveal (#474).

Jesus knew and loved us each and all during his life, his agony,
and his Passion and gave himself up for each one of us (#478).

Only the divine identity of Jesus' person can justify so absolutely a claim as "He who is not with me is against me"...and his
affirmations, "Before Abraham was, I AM"; and even "I and the
Father are one" (#590).

Jesus' violent death was not the result of chance in an unfortunate coincidence of circumstances, but is part of the mystery of
God's plan...(#599).

Christ's death is both the *Paschal sacrifice* that accomplishes the
definitive redemption of men...and the *sacrifice of the New*

Covenant, which restores man to communion with God by reconciling him to God through the "blood of the covenant, which was poured out for many for the forgiveness of sins" (#613).

This sacrifice of Christ is unique; it completes and surpasses all other sacrifices. First, it is a gift from God the Father himself, for the Father handed his Son over to sinners in order to reconcile us with himself. At the same time it is the offering of the Son of God made man, who in freedom and love offered his life to his Father through the Holy Spirit in reparation for our disobedience (#614).

What image or images of God are operating in these statements? What is the religious worldview? How valid is this religious worldview in the light of contemporary cosmology and the insights of contemporary scriptural scholarship?

Are we to keep telling a story about ourselves in relationship with God which views us primarily as a "fallen race"; has a male, localized God who reacts and locks us out, then sends his Son who walks this Earth knowing the "eternal plan"; and then has this Son dying a terrible, pre-planned death, so that we could be restored to friendship with this God? Will we keep quoting Scripture to back up this story without any reference to the worldview and thought patterns in which the Scripture writers and editors worked?

When a) ignorance of the way the Gospels were shaped and the way the Gospels wrote post-resurrection understanding back into the life of Jesus (especially John's Gospel); b) uncritical acceptance of the worldview in which both Scripture and doctrines were shaped; and c) centuries of rigorous intellectual defense of the proposition that Jesus is radically different from us because he is also the preexisting Son of God who lived in heaven before coming down to Earth, are put together it is no wonder that the human reality of Jesus became seriously neglected. Many Catholics read John's Gospel and understand Jesus to be fully aware that he is the Second Person of the Trinity because in the Gospel he speaks of "the Father and I." He is seen as the preexisting Word; he is understood as clearly knowing this and so Catholics over the centuries have quoted parts of this gospel and proclaimed: "See, Jesus *knew* he was God!" And the corollary, of course, is that he is not at all like us in our struggle to be human.

The task of setting Catholics free from traditionally ingrained ways of understanding the Gospels and the person of Jesus is not an easy one. First, these understandings are so deeply and strongly ingrained that they are perceived by some Catholics as basic truths, not able to be changed. Second, the changes to thinking require a process of adult education beyond the ten-minute homily on Sunday, and most Catholics are simply not willing to give time to this. Third, there is enormous resistance from ultraconservatives who see modern scriptural studies as a threat (which it is) to some of their entrenched views. Finally, official church teaching sometimes, as in the *Catechism*, ignores church scholarship and reflects a fundamentalist, literalist approach in the way it quotes Scripture and understands Jesus' role in human affairs. People of strong conservative inclination then quote these sources in an effort to undermine the integrity of men and women trying to present contemporary scholarship.

The breakdown of the religious worldview which shaped much of Christian traditional thought about Jesus presents a major challenge to all Christian churches: is there another story we could try telling in the light of today's knowledge, which could make sense of God's presence in our lives, our need for Jesus and salvation, and the role of the church in the world? Is there another way of understanding Jesus that is faithful to his role as savior, to his uniqueness, to his divinity, and to the need for a community we call "church"?

Yes, indeed there is!

NOTES

1. Thompson, William M., *The Jesus Debate: A Survey and Synthesis* (Mahwah, NJ: Paulist Press, 1985), p. 251.

2. Pontifical Biblical Commission; cf Fitzmyer, Joseph A. *Scripture and Christology: A Statement of the Biblical Commission with a Commentary* (Mahwah, NJ: Paulist Press, 1986), p. 48.

3. Pontifical Biblical Commission, *The Interpretation of the Bible in the Church*, p. 74.

4. Hick, John, *The Metaphor of God Incarnate: Christology in a Pluralistic Age* (Louisville, KY: Westminster John Knox Press, 1993), p. 2.
5. Dunn, James, *The Parting of the Ways* (London: SCM Press, 1991), p. 171.
6. Hick, op.cit., p. 41-42.
7. Thompson, op. cit., p. 249.
8. Küng, Hans, *Christianity* (London: SCM Press, 1995), p. 55. (See Bibliography for U.S. ed.)
9. Ibid., p. 96
10. Brown, Raymond, *Biblical Reflections on Crises Facing the Church* (London: Darton, Longman & Todd, 1975), p. 34. (See Bibliography for U.S. ed.)
11. LaCugna, Catherine M., "The Trintarian Mystery of God" in Fiorenza, Francis S. & John P. Galvin, eds., *Systematic Theology: Roman Catholic Perspectives* (Minneapolis, MN: Fortress Press, 1991), p. 160.
12. Dunn, op. cit., p. 244.
13. LaCugna, op. cit., p. 152.
14. Perkins, Pheme, *Gnosticism and the New Testament* (Minneapolis, MN: Augsburg Fortress Press, 1993), p. 3.
15. Kasper, Walter, *The God of Jesus Christ* (New York: Crossroad, 1992), p. 252.
16. LaCugna, op. cit., p. 168.
17. Macquarrie, John, *Jesus Christ in Modern Thought* (London: SCM Press, 1990), p. 383.
18. Wright, David, "Councils and Creeds" in *The History of Christianity: A Lion Handbook*, Tim Dowley, ed. (Tring, Herts, England: Lion Publishing, 1988), pp. 156-178.

REFLECTION

• What ideas in this chapter are new to me?

• What statements affirm my own thinking? How?

• Do some statements disturb my thinking? Why?

• Where do I stand in my understanding of salvation and redemption? the Trinity? Jesus as both human and divine? Incarnation?

RECOMMENDED READING

1. Brown, Raymond; *Responses to 101 Questions on the Bible* (Mahwah, NJ: Paulist Press, 1990). This book is a gem. It is very easy to read and will give readers new to scriptural scholarship a fascinating and enlightening introduction.

2. Goosen, Gideon & Margaret Tomlinson; *Studying the Gospels: An*

Introduction (Sydney: E. J. Dwyer, 1994). An easy-to-read, well-presented, yet scholarly book that would help a group or an individual explore contemporary understanding and approaches to the Gospels. 3. I have drawn heavily on James Dunn's book, *The Parting of the Ways.* This is not a book for general readership, but is most illuminating and interesting on the beginnings of Christianity and how Jesus was understood during those times. The book is based on lectures Dunn gave at the Gregorian Pontifical University in Rome from February through April of 1990.

CHAPTER SIX

Jesus Reveals the Sacred in Each of Us

Jesus lived most of his life in obscurity, emerged as a prophetic figure for several years, and was eventually crucified. After his death layer upon layer of interpretation and understanding was put on his life and his ministry so that it has become extremely difficult to get to know the flesh and blood reality of Jesus. Who did this man really think he was? What did he think he was doing? What did he hope to achieve?

We, two thousand years after he lived, tend to give answers to these questions that in all likelihood were not the human Jesus' answers. Our answers are the fruit of centuries of theological reflection. They are answers wrapped, inevitably, in particular thought patterns and worldviews, answers that depend on particular interpretations and understandings of the basic relationship between God and ourselves.

Our difficulty is that we begin with this later theological interpretation and understanding and read it *back* onto the historical Jesus.

What happens then is that the human reality of this man's life is distorted by approaching him through the lens of theological interpretation, rather than letting him be human like us and trying to see what we can learn about God and ourselves in the lived human experience of this man. The choice is whether our starting point in reflection on Jesus is that of the *Catechism*, as we saw in the previous chapter:

> By its union to the divine wisdom in the person of the Word incarnate, Christ enjoyed in his human knowledge the fullness of understanding of the eternal plans he had come to reveal... (#474).

or whether we start with someone who was human like us, and the realities of his life. The latter was the original starting point for Christian reflection. Two thousand years of reflection and interpretation, however, have put a cloak of understanding over the original reality, and we keep viewing Jesus in light of the cloak rather than reflecting on the original reality: Jesus' life and teaching. An example of this approach appeared in a review of a book about Jesus. The reviewer thought the author

> ...perhaps over compensates for the human Jesus of Nazareth. No one has ever managed to imagine the psychological consequences of the hypostatic union of God and human in Jesus Christ. One age swings one way, the next the other.
> We are in a "how human is Jesus" phase right now....[1]

What a pity that an attempt to come to grips with the reality of Jesus as thoroughly human like us is understood as a "phase" we are going through. And note the apparent need to understand Jesus through the lens of the "hypostatic union" rather than allow his humanity speak for itself.

Today, when we are at a crossroad of worldviews, it is vitally important that we return, with open minds, to Jesus' life to see what it reveals about the presence of the divine with us. Albert Nolan is one contemporary theologian who has made the human experience of

Jesus the basis for theological reflection about God. He writes:

> I have chosen this approach because it enables us to begin with
> an open concept of divinity and to avoid the perennial mistake
> of superimposing upon the life and personality of Jesus our pre-
> conceived ideas about what God is supposed to be like. The tra-
> ditional image of God has become so difficult to understand
> and so difficult to reconcile with the historical facts of Jesus' life
> that many people are no longer able to identify Jesus with that
> God. For many young people today Jesus is very much alive but
> the traditional God is dead.[2]

Let us leave aside the layers of theological interpretation that developed over the centuries and focus on the man Jesus and what we
know about his life and his preaching.

Jesus spent most of his life in Nazareth in Galilee. When we pon-
der what life there might have been like for Jesus, we find ourselves
asking questions such as: Who most influenced him in his religious
outlook? Who shaped his thinking? When did he begin to feel uneasy
or uncomfortable with the religious and social situations of his time?
When did he feel "called" to be a prophetic figure? How did that feel
for him?

In the past it has been easy enough to say, "Well, Mary would have
told him all about the Annunciation. Mary would have known he was
God and she would have shaped his upbringing accordingly." That
easy solution is no longer valid when we understand how "retrojection" is used by the Gospel writers. Who, then, had influence in shaping the religious thoughts and attitudes of this growing man?

Mary and Joseph would have been most influential, as any parents
are. It would help our understanding of Jesus if our thinking allowed
this couple to be normal and thoroughly human in their love for one
another and their love for Jesus. Surely it was from their expressed
love for him that Jesus developed his conviction that God is like a
most loving parent, to be absolutely trusted. Surely it was with Mary
and Joseph that Jesus at some stage of his growth into adulthood
began to ask questions about and discuss the religious and social

environment in which they lived. Apart from his parents, it seems that the Pharisees would have influenced Jesus significantly, and in a beneficial way.

This surprises us because our views on the Pharisees have been shaped by attitudes expressed in the Gospels of Matthew and John, where it appears there is no love lost between Jesus and the Pharisees. The Pharisees are the "bad guys." Again, we are dealing here with later attitudes being written back into the Gospel accounts. The antagonism with the Pharisees seems to be much more an early church issue than it was for Jesus personally.

Jesus was clearly influenced by the Pharisees' use of "Father" in reference to God, by their insistence that the sacred was accessible through acts of love and mercy, by their belief in the resurrection of the dead, and by their practice of shifting the emphasis in worship from the temple to the local community, in particular, to home settings. They were not tied to legalism, although it appears there were various divisions among Pharisees, with some groups being far more restrictive than others. The Pharisees would have nurtured the growing Jesus on "a new personal view of the Divine: a loving divinity (who) can be trusted to preserve our personal worth and dignity."[3]

We can only speculate how old Jesus might have been when serious questioning arose in him about the religious and social situation in which he lived. But we need to speculate. We need to see that this man wrestled with the conditions of his time, trying to decide what his response would be.

Like the prophets who lived before him, Jesus doubtless became aware of the gap between the ideals of a religious vision—a nation that would create a just society according to the norms of respect enshrined in the Ten Commandments—and the social reality of his time. He doubtless felt a "call" within him to stand up and be counted, to do something about the gap, to be a prophetic figure. But who, in his right mind, knowing what happened to prophets in former times, would ever put his hand up and volunteer to be a prophet!

How would a carpenter in Nazareth wrestle with this calling? What would his questions be? his doubts? his anxieties? What would he pray about? If we place the baptism of Jesus in the context of his personal questions, it takes on a new significance. The issue for Jesus is: stand up and be counted; let the Spirit of God have its way with you—completely. Give all your mind and heart and soul to the "call" within you. This is *conversion* in its most radical form. This is conversion where it hurts most.

THE ROOTS OF JESUS' MINISTRY

We can wonder (and this is fruitful prayer if we take time to do so reflectively) what thoughts and feelings might have occupied Jesus' mind and heart as he made his way to the Jordan River. What were the inner convictions that were driving him? Perhaps he sat on the bank of the river for quite a while before he stepped forward and committed himself to allowing the Spirit of God to have its way with him.

This was the beginning of Jesus' ministry. The preaching began and was accompanied by "deeds of power, wonders, and signs that God did through him among you…" (Acts 2:22). In Luke's Gospel we read,

> Then Jesus, filled with the power of the Spirit, returned to Galilee.…He began to teach in their synagogues and was praised by everyone. (4:14–15).

What was in Jesus' mind then? What were his expectations? What was he hoping to achieve? What were his dreams? The Gospel of Luke provides a scene from which we might derive some insights: Jesus returned to Nazareth where he was asked to read from "the scroll of the prophet Isaiah. Unrolling the scroll he found the place where it is written:

> The spirit of the Lord God is upon me,
>   because the Lord has anointed me
>   to bring good news to the poor.
> He has sent me to proclaim
>   release to the captives
> and recovery of sight to the blind,
>   to let the oppressed go free,

to proclaim the year of the Lord's favor (Lk 4:17–19).

If we were to imagine sitting down with Jesus after this event and asking him who did he think he was and what did he think he was doing, what do we imagine his answers might be? Was he nervous? afraid? super confident? confident of what? What did he expect the next couple of years to be for him?

N.T. Wright gives a good overview of the social, political, and religious background to Jesus' ministry. He mentions social unrest because of high taxes which bred resentment, frustration, and popular movements against the Romans. This background set up mounting expectations of a turnaround in which great changes for the good would take place.

This hope was enacted by all sorts of festivals, liturgies, and readings from sacred books. Pilgrimage to Jerusalem at Passover time in particular...a constant reminder that [God would rescue them again].... No more Romans, no more Herod, no more corrupt chief priests...simply God, a Messiah, and an Israel, devout, holy, and above all, free.[4]

Wright maintains that,

Jesus picked up this massive expectation—*and applied it to himself.*[5]

Jesus understood his ministry in terms of setting people free. We need to be clear about this. His life and death were not concerned with changing God's mind or winning back God's friendship. Rather, his living and dying were about changing people's minds and hearts. This is a different context in which to understand salvation. In Jesus' preaching, salvation is connected with setting people free from fear, ignorance, and darkness, and with changing the way they imaged and thought about God and themselves. In Luke's Gospel, the work of salvation is described in the Benedictus prayer of Zechariah, the father of John the Baptist:

> Blessed be the Lord God of Israel, for he has looked favorably on his people and redeemed them....that we would be saved from our enemies and from the hand of all who hate us...to grant us that we, being rescued from the hands of our enemies, might serve him without fear, in holiness and righteousness before him all our days....to give light to those who sit in darkness and in the shadow of death, to guide our feet into the way of peace (Lk 1:68–79).

Jesus' work of salvation directly addressed the issues of fear, ignorance, and darkness which clouded the religious thinking and images of the people.

In the Gospels, the collective term "crowd" is often used of the people. In Mark's Gospel the word for crowd (*ho ochlos*) is quite distinctive. It does not indicate only a large number of people, but also identifies those people as the lower class, the uneducated, the poor, known sinners, those ignorant of the law, and those alienated from the Jewish leadership. The rabbis taught that Jews should neither eat nor travel with these people.[6]

Jesus had his own terms and descriptions for these people whom he wanted to set free. In Matthew's Gospel we find Jesus wanting to minister not to "the righteous but sinners" (9:13). He felt sorry for the crowd for "they were harassed and helpless, like sheep without a shepherd" (9:36). His apostles were to minister to "the lost sheep of the house of Israel" (10:6). They were the people who "are weary and are carrying heavy burdens" (11:28).

The crowd included classes of people like shepherds, fishermen, tax collectors, and public sinners. Mark's Gospel presents the scandalous scene of Jesus, who "sat at dinner in Levi's house," where "many tax collectors and sinners were also sitting with Jesus and his disciples—for there were many who followed him" (2:15).

Then there were the sick, the maimed, the blind, the lepers, and the possessed. Bad enough for them to be on the bottom rung of society because of their physical misfortunes, but added to the physical suffering was the humiliating religious belief that their suffering could be God's punishment for sin. So in John's Gospel, Jesus' disciples ask him "Rabbi, who sinned, this man or his parents, that he was born blind?" (9:2).

While "the crowd" would have longed to see God's reign of justice and goodness, the people represented by this term had been conditioned by upbringing, social customs, and religious attitudes to believe that God was not near to them, that in fact their condition in life was clear evidence of God's displeasure.

Jesus named the real issue here: religious faith that is permeated by fear, ignorance, and a sense of distance from the sacred. It is in this context that he called people to conversion.

We need to be clear. Jesus' call to "Repent!" is not so much about a movement from personal sin to not sinning as it is about a change of mind and heart. It is about changing (converting) people's thoughts and images about God and how they see themselves in relationship with God. The call to conversion is the essential first step in order to believe good news: the kingdom of God is here among you. It is significant that in Mark, the earliest Gospel, the first words Jesus speaks, the words that set the agenda for his ministry, are: "The time is fulfilled, and the kingdom of God has come near; repent, and believe in the good news" (Mk 1:15).

Jesus addressed people who lived in fear of a God who could pull strings. Who knew what was around the corner when leprosy or blindness or illness could come as God's punishment for a relative's sin? His message seemed simple: you are to live with absolutely no fear of God. He gave images of the relationship that should prevail: you are to be like children in the arms of trusting parents; you are to call God "Daddy"; if God looks after the birds and the grass, how much more will God care for you.

And as for thinking about or imaging what God is like, again Jesus was radical: change your ideas and your images; God's nature is characterized by unbelievable graciousness, generosity, and mercy. He told stories to illustrate this, stories that would have made people's minds spin because the stories had such an extraordinary twist to them: a father who rejoices at the homecoming of a wayward son, a shepherd who carries a lost sheep home. Not only did he tell stories, he lived the reality, and scandalized the righteous by the way he befriended sinners and the lower classes, by his tolerance and readiness to be compassionate and forgiving.

To people of his day who could not move from rigorous concepts about "God's justice" and who objected that this was all too easy, Jesus told a story about workers in a vineyard: when those who had worked all day objected because those who came in late received the same wage, the vineyard owner replied, "Am I not allowed to do what I choose with what belongs to me? Or are you envious because I am generous?" (Mt 20:15).

Jesus no doubt encountered generosity among the poor in a way not evident among the rich, the powerful, and the oppressors. The issue was that the poor were not able to recognize that their very generosity was what enabled them to help make present the kingdom of God. They thought God was not close to them. Jesus called them to change this way of thinking. Convert! God IS here—in your loving, in your caring, in your generosity, in your visiting. And more! God is ALWAYS here, even when you are conscious of your failure, your sin, your low status in life, and when everything seems to be going wrong.

CONVERSION IN ACTION

Jesus set the foundations here for what would become a key Christian insight: God is love, and when you live in love, you live in God, and God lives in you (1 Jn 4:16). However, this foundation can stay at the level of a pious thought unless people are led to identify their everyday experiences of goodness and caring with God's presence among them, and do this consistently, faithfully, and confidently. This is what Jesus tried to help the crowd to do.

In his preaching about God and in the way Jesus related with people, three issues are significant in light of how his role and ministry would be interpreted in later centuries.

1. He clearly did not relate with the crowd as people who had

lost God's friendship or whom God had locked out or banished. On the contrary, he ministered to people who thought that God was not close to them and challenged them to change their thinking—radically.

2. His role in life was not to change an attitude in God, to change God's mind, as it were, bringing human beings back into God's friendship and opening the gates of heaven for us. His role was concerned with people changing *their* minds, the way they perceived the reality of God and their relationship with God.

3. Nowhere in his preaching or in his dealings with people is there the slightest hint of the original sin mentality that later became so pervasive in the church's worldview. The Gospel evidence of the way Jesus related with children coupled with his teaching about God surely suggests he would have been horrified by the idea of children being born into a state of utter separation from God.

But ultimately, why should anyone believe this Galilean prophet? For while his message was indeed good news, it failed to convince many people of his time. There are very few people we know of in his lifetime who converted. It may well have been, as Andrew Greeley maintains, that it was human apathy, cynicism, and fear that finally defeated Jesus and his message, just as these attitudes have broken up "every enthusiastic social movement the world has known."[7]

Conversion from our entrenched thinking patterns and lifetime images of how things are may well be the most difficult conversion process of all. For in the process of changing thinking and images comes the challenge to act out of a new perception of reality, a new faith. Move! Stand up and be counted! Be involved! Witness to what you are now being led to believe!

The difficulty is that the new perception of reality is initially not as cohesive or as systematized as the old vision. People see they should change, see that some of their long-held images and ideas are no longer valid in the light of preaching or learning, but want someone to package a whole new system of understanding for them. Living with mystery and unanswered questions and taking personal authority for their own convictions is a new experience. Today, as in Jesus' time, it is also easy for fear, excuses, or apathy to take over.

It is easy to imagine in Jesus' time a cynicism being present in reactions like: well, it might be fine for you, Jesus, to stand there and say all these lovely things about God and us. But what if you were a leper? What if you were blind and had been kicked around all your life? What if you were a woman forced into prostitution, or a mother whose children died at an early age? What would you then believe about God and love and not having fear?

The cynicism is also evident in the comment still heard in Catholic circles today: well, it was different for Jesus. After all, he was God. And the implication is that he did not really experience the human condition as we do. It is a convenient way of dismissing both Jesus and his message.

In reality, it is not easy to believe that God is close and loving and not to be feared when one's life is entangled in pain, suffering, tragedy, loneliness, brokenness, or failure. In such times, it is psychologically difficult to hang onto a faith perspective which brings hope and joy in our more pleasant days.

In this context we need to contemplate the passion of Jesus. It was not a burden God asked Jesus to bear to "make up" for our sins. It was not a price to be paid so that God would relent and allow us back into God's friendship. What image of God is at the heart of such thinking? No, the passion is rather the reality of where human existence led this man. And, like us, in the harsher realities of life his faith perspective was tested to the limits.

At the end of his life, there was no glory for Jesus, no resounding success. His dream was not realized. People simply did not convert. The powerful had their way with him. He broke down and cried over Jerusalem. In the garden the night before he died, he "began to be distressed and agitated" (Mk 14:33). Whipped, spat on, and mocked, he went to a shameful death abandoned by his friends. Feeling abandoned even by God, this man reached deep into himself and refused to despair, refused to give up hope, refused to budge from his conviction that God is ultimately good, gracious, and to be trusted absolutely.

Isn't this what faith is all about? The letter to the Hebrews urges Christians to look "to Jesus the pioneer and perfecter of our faith..." (12:2). What a pity that the Catholic tradition took its eyes off Jesus' struggle as he faced his death. What a pity that many Catholics still stand in suspicion of contemplating Jesus this way. The charge is: you are reducing Jesus to a wimp! You are denying he is God!

Which is more important: that I put up my hand and make the right credal statements about Jesus (and God and church and the pope), or that I contemplate Jesus on the cross and steadfastly decide that I, too, will live with the faith that sustained this man to his death? Is it not in choosing the latter that a person is set free from darkness and fear? Is this not the salvation described in the Benedictus prayer of Zechariah?

Salvation is not about Jesus getting us into heaven; it is about Jesus setting us free. Salvation is an exodus experience, a movement from being imprisoned to being set free, from being bound to being released from bonds, from darkness to light, from fear to trust, from ignorance to insight and understanding.

Where are we bound and imprisoned? The preaching of Jesus suggests that it is mainly in our ideas and images concerning God and our relationship with God, and religious attitudes and practices that result from them. Here is the battleground of conversion.

What would have to happen if we allowed ourselves, personally and on a community basis, to be "set free," to be converted by the message of Jesus?

For a start we would have to decide that:

• Never again would we step into or operate out of, thoughts, images, and attitudes that in any way make us fearful of God.

• Never again would we operate out of a worldview that imagines God as a cruel manipulator of the human condition.

• Never again would we ask, "Why is God doing this to me?" when things go wrong in life. That has always been the wrong religious question and has always provided a warped idea of God as the heavenly string-puller. You cannot trust that God absolutely.

• Never again would we allow our liturgy, our prayers, and our rituals to suggest that we are a people distant from God.

• Never again would we act out of attitudes that suggest that we are not much good, and that God could not be close to us because we are just ordinary people.

• Never again would we divorce good, decent, loving human experience from the arena of the sacred. We would recognize and name our loving as a sharing in God's self and a sign that God truly is intimately a part of who we are in our humanity.

• Never again would we allow authority to "lord it over us," but would require authority to affirm God's presence with us and be supportive as we try to live the challenges of witnessing to it in our lives.

• Never again would we operate out of a worldview that maintains we are born in a state of utter separation from God or that God turned God's back on us because we messed up paradise.

• Never again would we engage in rituals or devotions that seek to buy God's mercy or protection or favor.

All of these "never agains" are firmly grounded in the message of Jesus. They provide quite an agenda for us as individuals and as church.

UNDERSTANDING JESUS' DIVINITY

Also on the agenda is the need for honest, open discussion in Catholic circles about what we understand as the "divinity" of Jesus. We must face, discuss, and be open about valid questions such as: is Jesus someone primarily on God's side who came from somewhere else, "down" to us to "save" us, in the traditional sense in which people understand those words? Or is Jesus to be radically on the human side, a visible expression of God—as fully as any human person could allow God's presence to be made visible, taken up in death into the fullness of life in God, and in his living and dying revealing our potential and our direction? If the latter, what are the implications of this for our understanding of Jesus as "divine"? Do we have a share in this divinity?

When the accent is put on Jesus' divinity, as someone unlike us, we miss the whole point of his life. He was not trying to win back God's friendship or get us a place in heaven. He was desperately trying to get people to believe in God's loving presence with them. As we saw, he tried to "save" us by setting us free from thoughts and images about God that imprisoned us. He tried to be a light in the darkness. He tried to convince people that the sacred is to be found in everyday life—especially in our loving. There was only one commandment he gave us—to love in the way he loved—and he believed that in this we would discover the sacred in our midst.

However, once we approach Jesus from the human reality and absorb what we might learn from that, the accusations come thick and fast: are you daring to say that Jesus is not God? Are you saying he is not the Second Person of the Blessed Trinity? Are you suggesting that he did not know this? How can you call yourself a Catholic and write what you have written?

Unfortunately, there can often be no dialogue, no meeting of minds when this air of suspicion surfaces, because the questioner is unable to come to grips with the basic point that is being made: this is not an attack on Christian faith. It is an assertion that Christian faith has been packaged in a particular way, in particular thought patterns that have been set in concrete and that the time has come to re-examine, with open minds, the fundamentals of our faith and to try expressing them in ways that are relevant to today's worldview.

The whole point of Jesus' life is that a human person like us so lived life that other people believed they saw the divine operating in him. Two issues emerge from this. Firstly, in the human life of this man, we believe we discern insights into what God is like. What, then, do we learn about God from contemplating this man's life? Secondly, we are led to believe that in our own human experience of life we can discern the divine operating in us. What do we learn about God from contemplating our own lives? In Jesus' life, Albert Nolan discerns

—that our God does not want to be served by us, he wants to serve us;

—he does not want to be given the highest possible rank and status in our society, he wants to take the lowest place and to be without rank and status;

—he does not want to be feared and obeyed, he wants to be recognized in the sufferings of the poor and the weak;

—he is not supremely indifferent and detached, he is irrevocably committed to the liberation of mankind...

and concludes,

If this is not a true picture of God, then Jesus is not divine. If this is a true picture of God, then God is more truly human, more thoroughly humane, than any human being.[8]

We are led to conclude from contemplating Jesus' life and preaching that the divine and the human are intermingled, and that to see a human person live a totally loving, gracious life is to see the face of God. The Wisdom of God finds visible expression in human beings. Of course there is more to the reality of God than this, but if we do not proclaim and celebrate this basic insight about ourselves and where and how we experience the divine, we are not being faithful to the understanding that dawned on the first Christians at Pentecost.

This basic spirituality should have been defended and promoted by theology. Over the centuries, unfortunately, theology has been more concerned with issues such as the two natures in Jesus, his divinity as distinct from us, and the intricacies of the Trinity, than with the foundational Christian insight that human beings are charged with the Spirit of God. Andrew Greeley comments:

How many times, for example, we have heard someone say: "Do you still believe in the divinity of Jesus?" or "I can no longer accept the divinity of Jesus."

Note what has happened. A truth of faith has become an intellectual matter that is either the subject of an examination to determine whether one is orthodox...or a doubt about which one can endlessly agonize.

That is not, I would submit, what religion is all about. The proper question is not "What do we have to believe?" but rather "What light is shed on the uncertainties and agonies of human existence by the experience-producing pictures, stories, and images of our faith?"

I do not wish to suggest that it is pointless to worry over the metaphysical problem of how humanity and divinity are combined in a special way in Jesus....But I would contend that the basic religious question about Jesus is not "How is he different from the rest of us?" but "Can I live in the gloriously joyous worldview which Jesus came to share with us and which Christianity claims to have validated in the experience of the Easter event?"[9]

We cannot escape the need to interpret Jesus and theologize about him. The question is whether we will do this within a framework which maintains that God is radically separate from human beings and that we are a fallen race, or within a framework which is thoroughly incarnational and has God's presence totally permeating everything that exists.

There is a principle, long respected in Catholic philosophy and theology, stating (to put it in simple terms) that we should not have recourse to a more complicated and unnecessary explanation for something if it can be explained in simpler terms. The literal notion of God needing to become human in order to redress the harm of our first parents' "fall," and the consequent theorizing that God must be a trinity of persons in order for this to make sense goes against this principle.

THE BASIS FOR THE TRINITARIAN MODEL

Our present understanding of human development on this planet has no need for a God-person to come down from heaven and save us by winning back God's friendship and entry into God's presence. This is not to say that we had and have no need of salvation; nor is it in any way an assertion that Jesus is not uniquely savior for us who are

Christian. But as we have already seen, Jesus' role as savior can be understood in ways that are not dependent on an outmoded religious worldview.

What happened, though, is that having interpreted Jesus' role in human affairs the way it did, the Christian church developed its understanding of God as a Trinity. What we have here is a *model* for thinking about God, a model which tried to answer the religious questions of the time. There has always been the risk of the model being understood literally; that is, as if it were actually describing God. The real issue, of course, was how to make sense of Jesus if we have to think of him as actually being God.

The Christian Creed set this model in concrete: we believe in God the Father; we believe in God the Son; we believe in God the Holy Spirit. The difficulty then becomes that if you question this you cannot be Catholic or Christian. Look what is happening here with such an assertion: whether you are or are not a genuine Christian and/or Catholic has come to depend on an intellectual model for thinking about God, a model constructed to make sense of Jesus having both a divine and human nature, as someone radically unlike us.

Three clear issues demand attention when this happens:

• First, we need to recognize, as Catholic theology in its tradition reminds us, that human statements about God can never be actual descriptions of God. The reality of God will always remain beyond any images, words, model, or description used by men and women. It is essential to realize that the reality of God simply cannot be bound to Christian descriptions of what God is. All our Christian descriptions do is deal with Christians' experience of God's activity and try to make sense of it in the prevailing religious and scientific worldview.

• Second, what does it mean to be a Christian? Does examination of the historical interpretation of Jesus' role in human affairs mean that someone who raises questions about the literalness of God as a Trinity could not thereby be a Christian? Would not a better and truer criterion of whether a person is a genuine Christian be: does the message of Jesus find a home in your heart and are you prepared to live by the good news that enlightened people at Pentecost? Is not the spirituality, the vision of life and response, meant to be the true mark of whether someone is genuinely Christian—and Catholic?

• Third, with regard to the Trinity, Jesus, Mary his mother, and the apostles, St. Paul and all the early Christians had no such concept of Jesus. Can this understanding, which Christian scholarship is presenting to us today, be permitted to speak to us about what is essential to being a Christian or a Catholic?

The Catholic Church will certainly continue to interpret Jesus primarily as the Second Person of the Blessed Trinity, the Son of God, one in being with God, equal with God as Father and Spirit. It would be unrealistic to expect a dramatic, sudden change in this, granted this interpretation is so pervasive both in thought and liturgy. But will the other, radical (as in "belonging to our roots") interpretation also be allowed a hearing? Will the Catholic Church actively promote an understanding of Jesus as the Wisdom of God made present and visible in this human person?

In the trinitarian model, "conceived by the Holy Spirit" leads us to think primarily of Jesus, the Son of God, as a preexistent being totally separate from the human condition, who breaks into the human situation in a miraculous way and who will always be thought of as radically different from us. In the wisdom model, we will think of the presence of God—God's very spirit and wisdom—at work in the Hebrew people for centuries. We will appreciate and admire their determination to free themselves from slavery, to create a new society based on justice and compassion. We will remember the Spirit of God working through the prophets and in the faith of the poor. We will recall the genealogy in Matthew's Gospel, not as a literal list of Jesus' ancestors, but as a proclamation that these people and this society brought forth this man and his insights and his convictions. He was a Jew through and through. We will be anchored in human experience, and wonder at the reality of a God who over millions of years worked within and with the limitations of life on this planet. In a particular time, in a particular place, in a particular culture, and in a particular person—Jesus—the Wisdom of God took flesh and became visible.

In the trinitarian model Jesus is unique because he is really God, because of his role as Son of God in human affairs and because his message is God's message. In the wisdom model Jesus is unique because of the particular way he embodied the Wisdom of God as a human person, the way he allowed the Spirit of God to motivate and direct his life, and because his preaching about God set people free. The wisdom model leaves open for consideration the possibility that the Wisdom of God can take flesh and be visible in love and in all human beings, which is the message of Pentecost.

John Hick argues that "incarnation" should be understood as a metaphor for human life rather than be a term applied uniquely to Jesus. All human beings have the potential to "incarnate" or "live out" truths and values and love that reflect a divine reality at work in us.

[Jesus]…embodied within the circumstances of his time and place the ideal of humanity living in openness and response to God, and in doing so he "incarnated" a love that reflects the divine love. This epoch-making life became the inspiration of a vast tradition that has for many centuries provided intellectual and moral guidance to Western civilization…if it can be liberated from the network of theories—about Incarnation, Trinity and Atonement—which served to focus but now only serve to obscure its significance, that lived teaching can continue to be a major source of inspiration for human life.[10]

This way of understanding incarnation may help Christianity as it wrestles with modern-day questioning of the notion that life on this planet developed to a certain stage, then God came down from heaven to fix up the mess we humans had made. Jesus will still be proclaimed as sharing fully in God's spirit—as being divine—but our understanding of what divinity meant for him may help us as Christians to discover what it means for us to assert that we, too, share fully in the Spirit that moved him.

It may also help Christianity come to grips with other aspects of trinitarian theology that are being challenged today. The most basic criticisms are that trinitarian theology is too abstruse for most of the faithful, seems divorced from everyday life and spirituality, distorts the human reality of Jesus, has little foundation in Scripture, and is used by Christianity to make absolute claims about itself. In popular understanding and imagination, trinitarian theology has helped cement images of a localized, male Father-God who sends a unique, male Son-God "down" to our world.

On the factor of absolute claims, Sallie McFague comments:

> The scandal of uniqueness is absolutized by Christianity into one of its central doctrines, which claims that God is embodied in one place and one place only: in the man Jesus of Nazareth. He and he alone is "the image of the invisible God" (Col 1:15)....In its traditional form the claim is not only offensive to the integrity and value of other religions, but incredible— indeed, absurd—in light of postmodern cosmology. It is not remotely compatible with our current picture of the universe.[11]

In popular piety, the notions of three persons in one God and two natures in the person of Jesus have emphasized Jesus as totally different from us. The effect, asserts Monika Hellwig, has been to turn Jesus "into an alien among us who spent a while in exile for our sake and then left our planet and mode of existence to return to his own proper sphere."[12]

Let us try to place Jesus in the context of what we know today about development of life on this planet and in the context of a thoroughly incarnational concept of God. As we saw in Chapter Four, the thousand years before Jesus produced a worldwide development in human thought and reflection towards transcendence: a reality that is beyond the human and surrounded in mystery and awesomeness. Different peoples and groups and religions gave this reality different names and imaged it quite differently. The Jewish people had several names for it. We simply call it "God."

In terms of human development we really are still in the infancy stages of our understanding of this transcendent reality. We are still in the early stage of learning and believing that our very existence and meaning in life are bound up with God, that somehow human life and God are intertwined, and that this God at work in us can do far more than we dare ask or imagine (Eph 3:20). We have come to believe, as Christians, that after death there is a "fullness of life" to be experienced with God. We are occasionally in touch with, but probably do not nurture sufficiently, the deep yearning that seems to be in the hearts of all human beings to experience this reality beyond us. Our experiences of deep love suggest that in our loving we are somehow in touch with this transcendence, but we can never catch it or hold it. It is always greater than and beyond human experience.

John Macquarrie, in commenting on Jesus and his place in this process of human development, begins by stating that the "potentialities of humanity are still to unfold." Humanity will always be "more" than we think, and this "more" will unfold the more human beings walk on the path of transcendence, "toward the supreme mystery we call God."

> This, I believe, is of the highest significance for an understanding of the claims that have been made for Jesus Christ. To call him God-man (or whatever the preferred expression may be) is to claim that in him human transcendence has reached a point at which human life has become so closely united with the divine life that, in the traditional language, it has been "deified." It has not, however, ceased to be human—rather, for the first time, we learn what true humanity is.[13]

We cannot imagine what human life will be like 5000 years from now, but the crucial question for the well-being of this planet and our survival on it is: will we allow this mysterious transcendent reality to continue moving the human condition to greater heights? Or will we allow fear, apathy, cynicism, our thirst for power and profit, our selfishness, our crude self-seeking materialist outlook, our refusal to share the goods of the earth, and all those other attitudes that indicate the reality of sin in human endeavor to dictate the course ahead for human beings on this planet?

Jesus offers us extraordinary insights into the nature and presence of the transcendent reality we Christians name as "God." He offers life-giving insights about the manner of our relationship with God, with all of creation, and with each other. All of this must have significant impact on the way Christians try to influence society and decisions that affect the well-being of life on this planet. We who profess to be thoroughly Christian would do well to listen to and promote Jesus' message of salvation in ways that link it primarily with *this* world, not the world to come. Our theologizing about Jesus could then be linked with a spirituality that affirms the incarnation of God's wisdom, love, and spirit in all of creation and in each of us.

Let us defend the absolute, certain human reality of Jesus, and let terms such as "divinity," "in the image of God," "sons and daughters of God," "sharing the Spirit of God," and "sharing God's life" be for us not only mysterious and beyond imagining, but also wonderful, hopeful, affirming, creative, and courageous as we work to establish God's kingdom on earth.

NOTES

1. Boland, T., *The Catholic Leader,* Queensland, 3rd September, 1995.

2. Nolan, Albert, *Jesus Before Christianity* (Maryknoll, NY: Orbis Books, 1978), p. 136.

3. Thompson, *The Jesus Debate,* p. 160.

4. Wright, N.T., *Who Was Jesus?* (Grand Rapids, MI: William B. Eerdmans Publishing Company, 1993), p. 94.

5. Ibid., p. 100.

6. Myers, Ched, *Binding the Strong Man: A Political Reading of Mark's Story of Jesus* (Maryknoll, NY: Orbis Book, 1988), p. 156.

7. Greeley, Andrew, *The Jesus Myth* (London: Search Press, 1972), p. 55.

8. Nolan, op. cit., p. 138.

9. Greeley, Andrew, *The Great Mysteries: An Essential Catechism* (Minneapolis, MN: The Seabury Press, 1976), pp. xiv-xv.

10. Hick, *The Metaphor of God Incarnate,* pp. 12-13.

11. McFague, *The Body of God,* p. 159.

12. Hellwig, Monika, *Jesus, the Compassion of God: New Perspectives on the Tradition of Christianity* (Collegeville, MN: Michael Glazier, Inc., 1983), pp. 35-36.

13. Macquarrie, *Jesus Christ in Modern Thought,* p. 370.

REFLECTION

• Which of the "never agains" listed (pp.85-86) do I have to confront? What other "never agains" would I add?

• "We cannot deduce anything about Jesus from what we think we know about God; we must now deduce everything about God from what we do know about Jesus....To say now suddenly that Jesus is divine does not change our understanding of Jesus; it changes our understanding of divinity" (Nolan, p. 137). Has my reflection on Jesus changed my understanding of divinity?

• "...rather, for the first time, we learn what true humanity is." What am I learning about "true humanity"?

RECOMMENDED READING

1. Andersen, Frank; *Jesus, Our Story* (see Bibliography for U.S. edition). Very suited for personal reflection and prayer.

2. Nolan, Albert; *Jesus Before Christianity;* and Thompson, William; *The Jesus Debate.* Either or both would be ideal for a study or discussion group approach.

CHAPTER SEVEN

A Radical Spirituality

What do we mean by "spirituality"? We each have our images and thoughts about God and our relationship with God. Spirituality is simply the manner in which we allow these images and thoughts to direct the way we live. We can, for example, picture God as a cruel dictator. That belief would have an enormous impact on our relationship with God, our style of prayer and worship and self-image.

We could, on the other hand, perceive God as incredibly loving and understand ourselves as being richly blessed with the presence of God's Spirit. Obviously, in the second example, our spirituality will be quite different from the first example. What we believe and image and the way this influences the way we live, relate, pray, and worship—this is our spirituality.

As Catholics, our spirituality has been shaped and packaged for us by centuries of experience, thought, and reflection. We inherited a Catholic worldview at an early age. We took this on board, unquestioningly in most cases, and tried to be faithful to it.

One of the problems being encountered today—and one we *must* face if our spirituality is to be real—is that much of our inherited spirituality was shaped by religious thought patterns and worldviews that are now questionable, if not irrelevant. It is somewhat like trying to perform heart surgery in a modern hospital with only the knowledge of fifteenth-century medical science. It is not that anyone wants to scoff at the medical knowledge of earlier centuries. That would be unfair. Likewise with our religious worldview and our spirituality. The intent is not to belittle earlier thought patterns which sustained Christian living for centuries. The intent is rather to look at the basics of our religious beliefs in the light of today's worldview which is vastly different from that which shaped Christian thought in its beginnings. What we find is good news: the Christian message blends beautifully with today's worldview.

Christianity has always maintained that God is infinite, that God is everywhere, that God's presence sustains everything that has existence. If we pay more attention to this dimension of Christian understanding about God, we will develop a spirituality that is more relevant in our age.

Let us return to the realities of space, time, and distances mentioned in Chapter Two to release our image of God from the straitjacket in which it has been shaped. Let God in our thought and in our images be the God of 400 billion galaxies (and even possibly of other universes beyond this one). Let God be everywhere. And let us take that seriously: *everywhere.* Let God be the God of this expanding universe, and far beyond. For too long we have given lip-service to this truth about God while in our spirituality we have retreated into the localized overseer, big Daddy-looking-down-on-us image.

As we saw in Chapter Three, God is that Infinite Being who is the source and sustainer of all life. God is indeed *in* all, *with* all, and *through* all that has existence. God is not more present to one being than another. God is not "in" any one person more than God is "in" another person. No: God permeates all creation.

Let us pause and examine what this means for a spirituality.

It surely suggests that we must rid ourselves of notions that we have to buy or win God's love or presence. God's presence is an essential condition for existence. You cannot have "more" or "less" of it.

Every one of us is permeated with God's presence. The pope does not have it any more than the truck driver or the nurse. The vital difference comes not from the reality but from the recognition and the naming of the reality, that is, naming and recognizing oneself as someone who gives flesh to, gives human form to, gives a particular, unique, personal human expression to the reality we name as God. God comes to expression, comes to a particular life form in ME. In me, God can speak, can move, can dance, can compose music or write poetry, can make love and create life, can laugh and can cry at the imperfection of it all.

The reality we name as "God," mightier and more vast than 400 billion galaxies, permeates my existence as a human person. Certainly God is infinite and unknowable; but we look into our own hearts and lives, and there is this same God bursting to life in us. Why do we keep looking elsewhere to find God? Why do we stay locked into a spirituality that looks for God in the heavens in preference to a spirituality that focuses on the God within and among us, urging and prompting us to claim our sacred identity—and to live it? Here is the arena of conversion and the heart of Jesus' message to all of us who have ears to listen.

Our spirituality needs to articulate more clearly and more thoroughly this basic relationship between God and ourselves. It should emphasize both the reality of God's presence with us, and our responsibility to allow that presence to emerge and be seen in the way we live. Our basic sin, if we are to talk about an "original sin," is our blindness to this reality of who we are and the ways we block the emergence of the sacred within us. The story is not of a "fall" from a perfect state of consciousness and developed conscience; rather, it is the story of the slow emergence within human beings of the realization that the sacred is deep within each of us.

Bede Griffiths gives an overview of stages in the development of human consciousness:

1. A stage of primeval consciousness when human beings were totally immersed and one with nature.

2. About 200,000 BC, the beginning of separation along with development of consciousness of the body.

3. About 50,000 BC, the development of language. This was an extraordinary breakthrough as it broke the bondage to the "concrete and the present." Recalling the past as well as planning for the future became possible in communication, and with this came the ability to better control the environment. About 10,000 BC saw the movement from just hunting (locked into the present) to agriculture (planning for the future).

4. The development of symbolic imagination in a time when people experienced themselves surrounded by spirits and "powers" and "presences."

5. The change to and development of social structure. Storing of food, the growth of cities, exchange and barter, the use of money. A leisure class emerged, and with this class developed writing, observation of the stars, the calendar. Much of this developed in the arena of religion since worship of the gods was at the center of life.

6. Later than 1000 BC, the development of logical thought, and with this the rise of the "hero myth" and the rise of patriarchy. Philosophy flourished and along with it the development of the ego and control of the world.[1]

We are still in the last-mentioned stage. In it we have viewed ourselves as "masters" of natural resources and done enormous damage to the ecological system of this planet. The tragedy is that much of this happened with the support of a religious outlook which proclaimed that we, as superior beings on this planet, could use the rest of creation as we liked.

The question a genuine spirituality must address is: where is God in all of this human development? Are we to imagine the Grand Designer out there somewhere, rearranging the building blocks, deciding, "Ah, now is the time to slip in separation from nature" and later, "Let's see how they get on if I give them logical thought"?

Can we, will we, move away from such ways of imaging God and take seriously the notion that God is intertwined IN this development? What we see then is God limited by what God has to work with, and that insight and understanding come slowly in the process of human development. The pattern is one of slow, patient development as human consciousness struggles with meaning, purpose, its capacity for both good and evil, and its sense of a transcendent reality that we Christians name "God."

God is in the development, in its slowness, its messiness, and in its peaks of insight. At the very heart of Christian belief we have this insight into the mystery of God: God is not an unchanging, aloof reality; God truly is part of the ebb and flow of life and all that has existence.

GOD WORKING IN AND THROUGH ALL

For millions of years the reality of God moved in and through this universe of ours. Then here on this small planet in this particular galaxy, life began (or could we say, God expressed God's self in particular life forms) and developed and adapted to a point where life became, in human beings, capable of conscious awareness and reflection, of rational decision and choice, of love. Life reflected in this marvelous way the very reality of God: life in the image of God!

Reflect on who we are: this infinite reality we name as God comes to lived expression in each of us. Will we put our faith in this basic truth about God and ourselves, about who we are, and how the gift of life calls us to give expression to this? The issue for spirituality is whether we see ourselves as "poor, banished children of Eve" or as the dwelling places of the sacred. Which will we reflect in the way we pray, worship, and behave?

Will we use this conviction of God's presence permeating all reality to rid ourselves of the harm dualism has caused in Christian thought and attitudes in setting one over the other: heaven-earth; soul-body; spirit-flesh; head-heart; sacred-secular; Catholic-

Protestant; Christian-Jew; divine-human? God is not more present in one than in the other.

Will we also use this conviction to regain a sense of our connectedness with the rest of creation, a deeper appreciation of being nurtured into existence and being dependent on life forms and an ecological system that still nurtures us in existence? Will we respect the presence of God in it? Will we, as Christians, make our sacred respect visible and active in voicing concern on environmental issues?

Revelation, as we have seen earlier, is not about an external, distant Godhead deigning to break the silence or having second thoughts about friendship with us. Revelation is all around us. All of creation is part of the revelation of God.

In human beings, revelation has been and always will be tied to God being given a voice, coming to expression in particular places, in particular cultures, with particular thought patterns and worldviews, and in particular people. This calls us to move away from a spirituality of exclusiveness. The notion of a Godhead based in the heavens talking only to a particular group of people has been very much part of the Jewish and Christian traditions and basic to their understanding of revelation and their self-identity. The challenge now is coming to terms with an image of God that is not so limiting.

This challenge also holds the possibility of better dialogue with other religions. Rather than communicating from positions of exclusivity—we have God on our side; we have the truth and you haven't—dialogue could be along these lines: as we listen and pay attention to the reality of God in our cultures and our worldviews and our experiences, these are the insights we have come to. We realize we cannot contain the notion of God in our limited worldviews, but we offer our insights to you for your consideration. At the same time, we wish to learn from your experiences and insights for we believe God is working in and through all of us.

On the point of exclusivity, there is also a far broader issue. Our knowledge of this universe is still very limited. We have no knowledge of what life forms may have developed in some distant galaxies. And we are still arrogant in our assumptions that we human beings are THE centerpiece of all of creation, that conscious, reflective life forms could not develop elsewhere. (The redemption model has been largely responsible for limiting Christian thinking here. What if life forms on another planet sinned? Would God's Son have to "go down" to redeem them? It shows how a particular way of imaging reality has locked up our thinking.) We have not had to face the reality yet, but at least we need to shape a spirituality that can embrace the possibility of God at work, with rational life forms developing elsewhere.

Many people today—and this is not confined to Christianity—live a spirituality that is based on belief in an overseeing deity who rewards and punishes; when things go wrong in life, the explanation is that God must be testing or punishing them. Within Catholic circles it is commonplace to hear people speak of God asking them to carry a cross or that it must be "God's will" if tragedy occurs. The punishing God image is also still very much alive.

Our spirituality might well become much healthier if, especially in difficult times, we substituted the words "life" or "reality" for "God." Life does ask me to bear a cross occasionally. Reality is testing. What does "life" ask of us in the midst of enormous pain and tragedy? And whatever it asks, can we believe God is in the reality, rather than perceive God as a far-off overseeing deity asking something difficult of us?

Jesus provides new images of ourselves and God which are meant to be good news for us: God is here; God loves unconditionally—now! God is not to be feared. After his death the New Testament writers expressed the basics of Christian spirituality. It is these basics that remain constant while culture, worldview, and even our images of God change. If we are to have a genuine Christian spirituality, we must be able to link our understanding of God, Jesus, and ourselves in ways that are faithful to Jesus' preaching and the New Testament.

One of the foundation stones for this understanding is provided in the letter to John: God is love and when you live in love you live in God and God lives in you (1 Jn 4:16). We must believe of ourselves that the sacred which we name as God is intimately part of each of us, and love is the expression we give to it. So let us have a down-to-earth spirituality that proclaims that the kitchen, the workplace, the garden, the community center, and the bedroom—as well as the parish church and the tabernacle—are permeated with the presence of God. And let us proclaim the good news that ordinary people, struggling and battling to be faithful to their commitments and responsibilities, are no less God-filled than the greatest of saints, for we dare to believe that God is love and when you live in love you live in God and God lives in you.

Let us believe, as did the early Christians following Pentecost, that the *same* Spirit of God that moved in Jesus moves in us. And again, let us be sure about this: we are not talking about a difference in kind or quality or even quantity. The Spirit of God permeates us just as it permeated Jesus 2000 years ago. The key difference is that he recognized the reality and allowed that Spirit to have its way with him whereas Catholic spirituality, as many people seem to live it, is wary of believing that we, too, are filled with the same Spirit of God.

We must, in other words, reclaim the truth of Pentecost. We can state it this way: if you believe that Jesus in his lifetime made visible what God is like because of the way he allowed God's Spirit to work in his life, then you must also believe that the very same Spirit is at work in you. We are to be the people who continue what he did. This is what "church" is. It is about people who believe they are Spirit-filled, called to continue and spread the good news that has its source in the life and preaching of Jesus.

Scripture is clear—and challenging: "Examine yourselves to see whether you are living in the faith. Test yourselves. Do you not realize that Jesus Christ is in you?—unless, indeed, you fail to meet the test!" (2 Cor 13:5).

One of our constant stumbling blocks is that we do not try to get beyond scriptural statements, or are not helped to get beyond them. We need to bring the text above, and many others, into everyday life and everyday language. What, for example, does it mean for a mother of six children or a truck driver struggling to support their families to be told "Jesus is really in you"? Isn't it a fact of Catholic living that most Catholics would not identify either the language or the reality it is trying to portray with their own lives? The typical response is more likely to be along the lines, "Who? Me? You've got to be kidding." This sort of response is also to be found among religious and clergy as well.

Only when we Catholics can articulate what we mean by saying "Jesus lives in me" *and* believe what we are saying can we have a genuine Christian spirituality. Without this we can have religion and loyalty and adherence to doctrines, but we haven't got a genuine Christian spirituality.

St. Paul stated that "...it is no longer I who live, but it is Christ who lives in me" (Gal 2:20). They are words most Catholics have heard all their lives. But again the reality is that many Catholics think they are words that have relevance only for religious fanatics or the great saints.

A challenge to all Catholics, and indeed to all Christians, is this: whatever you say about Jesus in his lifetime sharing the Spirit of God, say about yourself. Immediately this would be perceived by some people as blasphemous. Why? Because Jesus was God!

Can we see what is happening here?

The immediate response is to perceive Jesus as radically different from us. This perception dominates popular Christian thinking. Consequently, the Christian message gets blocked at its roots: Christians will not seriously consider the reality and the implications of "the life of Jesus who lives in us" when Jesus is primarily thought of as a God-figure. We cannot possible be as courageous as Jesus-God.

A NEW VISION OF LIFE

The inability of Catholics to understand and identify with the basic message of Pentecost is one of the most basic issues to be addressed in the Catholic Church. What if, with Paul, we strove to ensure that Catholics believed with great conviction that they are "God's temple, and that God's Spirit dwells in you" (1 Cor 3:16)? Wouldn't the long-term results be very fruitful through personal affirmation, liturgical celebration, and more widely accepted ownership of being church?

One major stumbling block is the deep-seated attitude that what we believe about God, Jesus, church, the pope, or a particular doctrine is more important than what we believe about ourselves. Correct doctrinal thought and obedience to church laws and practice have had far more attention in the formation of Catholics than a spirituality affirming their own sacredness. It produced loyal church members, but it also limited the capacity and freedom of God's Spirit.

St. Paul set out to affirm in people that the same Spirit that moved in Jesus moved in them and that it was now their task to keep that Spirit visible in many differing ways. This highlights the task facing today's church community: affirmation of the sacred in the lives of all people. This must be done persistently, insistently, and consistently. It is not enough just to touch on affirmation occasionally. It must become a feature of preaching and of liturgy again and again and again if we are to break through into people's lived experience and free entrenched attitudes that prevent them hearing the good news.

Only then, like Paul, will the church community have the right to challenge people to give witness to what they believe about themselves. If the affirmation and the belief are not there, we can forget the challenge. Yet this is one of the major mistakes the church community is making on all levels today in asking people to take on tasks and responsibilities and decision making without grounding them in a solid spirituality.

If we want to see how this spirituality works in practice and works wonders in the lives of ordinary people, we only have to go back to the time of Paul's preaching. Paul convinced people that there was a "new creation," founded on the reality of everyone being part of the Body, everyone a bearer of the Spirit of God, and that NOW was the time to let the fruits of the Spirit be seen. With this vision of life, Paul led the break from centuries of dependence on law.

Central to the spirituality being outlined here is the belief that divinity is not a reality that exists only "in heaven," or that the reality we name as "God" is a reality existing somewhere else. The reality of God permeates our existence. Humanity, like the rest of creation, is saturated with divinity. The unique wonder of humanity is that it can reflect on and appreciate this truth. If human beings did this, they might work at creating the kingdom of God as Jesus saw it could be and as the church wants it to be, "a kingdom of truth and life, a kingdom of holiness and grace, a kingdom of justice, love, and peace" (Preface for the Feast of Christ the King). But we will never create that kingdom among us if we keep holding to a spirituality that proclaims that God and divinity are realities somewhere else, and while our theology constantly emphasizes that Jesus was radically different from us—because he was divine!

And if this perspective opens up difficult and awkward questions for traditional theology and its worldview and for the spirituality that had its birth in that worldview, then so be it. And if we have to move from the security of having all the answers in neat theological formulas, then so be it. And if we have to live with more ambiguity and mystery than before, then so be it. And if we have to admit as Christians that we only have partial insight into the reality of God, and that our insights are necessarily bound to and conditioned by time and place and language and culture and thought patterns and cosmology, then let us do so.

On the other hand, we believe as Christians that through Jesus we have wonderful insights into the relationship between God and human beings. This is good news for us, and we are moved to share this good news because we believe it has the potential to change peoples' lives and relationships for the good. We believe it offers an understanding of human existence that answers some of the most basic questions people have asked about life and its purpose. We also believe that we can articulate our insights and understandings in ways that conform with contemporary scientific understanding of the world and the universe. The Christian message stands the test of time and great changes. It is ready to face any changing worldview. It seems a pity that Christianity in its face to the world does not exhibit such confidence.

The insights and good news that our spirituality should be keeping alive and promoting are found in the witness of the early Christian communities. What were their convictions that can act as criteria for a genuine Christian spirituality for us? They are clear, uncompromising, and challenging:

• They believed that the spirit of God moved in them and wanted to move in them as courageously as that same spirit had moved in the human Jesus.

• Their remembrance of Jesus was not so much focused on the past, but on the NOW. The power of the Risen Christ working in and among them was an awesome power. They gave witness to this presence. They were the presence of the Christ in the world.

• The sacred was found, encountered in their midst.

• They were totally committed to radical equality.

• They were totally committed to service. They had a radical approach to WHO was to exercise authority and the WAY authority was to be exercised. Central to understanding this was their belief in themselves as "the Body of Christ" and that no one had any right to lord power over the Body the way pagans lorded power.

• Hospitality and greeting were a feature of the way this Body came together in their communities.

• They had insights into what God is like and who Jesus is, and these insights had to be communicated.

• There was radical equality in the way they ritualized Jesus' presence among them in the Eucharist. For the sake of "holy order" someone from the community presided, but he was not a person set apart from the normal life of the community. It would have been unthinkable for them to have a Christian community and not be able to designate someone in that community to preside at the community's eucharist.

• Eucharist and Christian living were inescapably connected with concern for the poor. The prophets in the Old Testament made it clear that God is not interested in ritual or sacrifice as such. In Amos we read the rebuke: "I hate, I despise your festivals...Even though you offer me your burnt offerings and grain offerings, I will not accept them....Take away from me the noise of your songs....But let justice roll down like waters, and righteousness like an everflowing stream" (5:21–24).

A challenging question for Catholics today is whether our parish communities, as communities, are distinguishable from the general attitudes of society towards the really poor in our midst. Bernard Cooke in a public address asked whether Catholicism has "lost its soul."[2] His point was that as Catholics have moved up the ladder of economic success they have, in general, accepted uncritically today's social attitudes towards the disadvantaged. Yes, Catholics give generously to appeals, but the effective power and compassion of God has to be seen working against the political, social, economic, and even religious powers that disadvantage people in systematic ways.

Much of our moral focus as Catholics has been on individual morality. While that focus will remain, we are being challenged today to focus also on social systems and economic strategies which manipulate, exploit, and dehumanize. The effective power and compassion of God has to be embodied, and Eucharist proclaims that we will be this presence. If Eucharist does not lead us to this awareness and action, then our Eucharists are a sham.

THE PLACE OF PRAYER

Alongside our participation in Eucharist, we need personal prayer to deepen our convictions.

Many Christian adults remain fixed at a level of prayer that offers little chance for their spirituality to deepen. Most of us learned as children that prayer is talking to God. When, as adults, people stay at that level of understanding, prayer is mainly concerned with speaking to God, asking God for favors, or thanking and praising God. No one would want to criticize these forms of prayer. However, there is also the prayer of reflection and of contemplation, and many Christian adults never have the opportunity to be nurtured into the practice of these prayer forms. These prayer forms require some silence, some slowing down of the mind, and a sensitivity to the movement of our hearts and moods.

One way to pray is to sit in silence with a passage from Scripture and allow it to speak to us personally. This is clearly in contrast with a prayer form that fills up the time speaking to God.

Another form of prayer that many people find helpful is prayer that engages both the human heart of Jesus and our own hearts. We could take a Gospel story and imagine what it was like for Jesus, responding to his invitation to know his heart. This helps us to image Jesus as more human, and very much like us in the events of his life. We can also take time to sit quietly and be present to the moods of our own hearts, naming and owning what is there, being real with ourselves, and then asking Jesus if he had ever felt like this.

These two types of prayer help us build empathy and friendship between Jesus and ourselves. They help us descend into the realities of our own hearts and remain there for a while; they lead us to greater compassion. This compassion and understanding is first between Jesus and ourselves—because our hearts and our human experiences have common ground—leading to greater compassion towards ourselves. In turn, our prayer leads us to bring the compassion and understanding of Jesus' heart to others.

Another form of prayer that many people find helpful is to focus on the reality that we are temples of God's Spirit, allowing that truth to touch both our heads and our hearts and enabling it to draw some significant response from us.

There is a self-contemplative aspect to each of these forms of prayer, that is, the prayer puts us more in touch with the sacred which is present and operating in our own lives. Our task in prayer is to grow in awareness of this reality. Indeed, if our prayer life is not helping us to grow in this awareness, then there is something radically in need of change in our prayer.

St. Paul says we human beings hold a "treasure in clay jars" (2 Cor 4:7). Sometimes men and women, confronted by the reality of life, move into the depths of their being, and there surfaces a courage, love, care, commitment, and fidelity they did not know (and others did not suspect) they were capable of. Their hidden self grows strong. They find a power within them that moves them to achieve far more than they could have dared ask or imagine. We human beings are capable of manifesting quite extraordinary depths of love and fidelity. It would be a great shame if, acknowledging this reality of love and courage that is within each of us, we did not give it its proper name: when we live in love, we live in God, and God lives in us. On the other hand, a clay jar has its cracks and bruises. We fail; we do wrong. We need to know that in prayer we can confront and own our failure and discover that the treasure has not departed. We turn to it, trying to develop awareness of it again, trusting that it will have greater influence on our actions in the future.

It is possible, however, for the clay jar to be so twisted and distorted by a person's wrong or evil choices that the treasure within is not enabled to surface. It's there. But God can only work with what God has to work with. God is in all "human vessels," but God is dependent.

This truth is beautifully captured in this passage by Antoine de Saint-Exupéry, author of *The Little Prince*. The setting is a train journey de Saint-Exupéry took before the start of the second world war. The first class carriages were empty, while the third class carriages were crowded with Polish workmen being sent home from France:

Looking at them I said to myself that they had lost half their human quality. These people had been knocked about from one end of Europe to the other by the economic currents....

A baby lay at the breast of a mother so weary that she seemed asleep. Life was being transmitted in the shabbiness and the disorder of this journey. I looked at the father. A powerful skull as naked as a stone. A body hunched over in uncomfortable sleep, imprisoned in working clothes, all humps and hollows. The man looked like a lump of clay, like one of those sluggish and shapeless derelicts that crumple into sleep in our public markets.

And I thought: The problem does not reside in this poverty,

in this filth, in this ugliness. But this same man and this same woman met one day. This man must have smiled at this woman. He may, after his work was done, have brought her flowers. Timid and awkward, perhaps he trembled lest she disdain him. And this woman, out of natural coquetry, this woman sure of her charms, perhaps took pleasure in teasing him. And this man, this man who is now no more than a machine for swinging a pick or a sledgehammer, must have felt in his heart a delightful anguish. The mystery is that they should have become these lumps of clay. Into what terrible mould were they forced? What was it that marked them like this as if they had been put through a monstrous stamping machine? A deer, a gazelle, an animal grown old, preserves its grace. What is it that corrupts this wonderful clay of which man is kneaded?

I sat down face to face with one couple. Between the man and the woman a child had hollowed himself out a place and fallen asleep. He turned in his slumber, and in the dim lamplight I saw his face. What an adorable face! A golden fruit had been born of these two peasants. Forth from this sluggish scum had sprung this miracle of delight and grace.

I bent over the smooth brow, over those mildly pouting lips, and I said to myself: This is a musician's face. This is the child Mozart. This is a life full of beautiful promise. Little princes in legends are not different from this, protected, sheltered, cultivated, what could not this child become?

When by mutation a new rose is born in a garden, all the gardeners rejoice. They isolate the rose, tend it, foster it. But there is no gardener for men. This little Mozart will be shaped like the rest by the common stamping machine. This little Mozart will love shoddy music in the stench of night dives. This little Mozart is condemned. I went back to the sleeping car. I said to myself: Their fate causes these people no suffering. It is not an impulse to charity that has upset me like this. I am not weeping over an eternally open wound. Those who carry the wound do not feel it. It is the human race and not the individual that is wounded here, is outraged here. I do not believe in pity. What torments me tonight is the gardener's point of view. What torments me is not this poverty to which after all a man can accustom himself as easily as to sloth....What torments me is not the humps not the hollows not the ugliness. It is the sight, a little bit in all these men, of Mozart murdered.

Only the Spirit, if it breathe upon the clay, can create Man.[3]

What we want a genuine spirituality to achieve is the "gardener's point of view": we nurture the divine presence in ourselves; we act conscious of being embodiments of that divine presence for others; we nurture and respect that presence in others; we commit ourselves to work with others for the sake of making that presence more visible in our social and economic structures; we respect and nurture the way that presence permeates all of creation.

NOTES

1. Griffiths, *A New Vision of Reality*, pp. 33-48.
2. Cooke, Bernard, "Eucharist and the Call to Justice," public address at Boston College, July 23, 1996.
3. de Saint-Exupéry, Antoine, *Wind, Sand and Stars* (Cutchogue, NY: Buccaneer Books, 1992), pp. 226-229.

REFLECTION

• What would I list as four or five foundational beliefs shaping a genuine Christian spirituality?

• What do I understand by saying, "it is Christ who lives in me"? When do I make this most evident?

• What have been turning points in my growth into a healthy spirituality?

• What is it we are doing when we attend Eucharist?

• What do I look for in my experience of church involvement to sustain me in a healthy spirituality? What is already in place? What is lacking? What more would I like to be involved in?

CHAPTER EIGHT

Leadership in a New Millennium

A striking feature of the tasks facing church leadership in a new millennium is how similar they are to those which faced early church leadership: helping Christians to focus on Jesus and his teaching about God, helping them to be aware of the presence of God's Spirit within and among them, and challenging them to give strong witness to the presence of that Spirit by their manner of living. Another similarity is the reality of dramatically changing times with a strongly established and well-institutionalized religious worldview being turned on its head. In such times what we focus on will either help us cope and grow or will divide, distract, and disappoint us.

Our focus now, as always, should be on our foundational Christian beliefs about God, Jesus, and ourselves:

1. God is everywhere. God is beyond whatever images we have of God; God is life-giving, loving, unbelievably compassionate; God is not to be feared, but to be trusted absolutely.

2. Jesus as a human person made the reality of God visible for people. In this man's living and loving we know God has been embodied. In God raising this man into the fullness of God's life we see our own destiny. Jesus gives meaning to who we are, and shows us our potential as human beings to let the image of God be seen in us.

3. Because of Jesus and resurrection and Pentecost we dare to believe that we are sons and daughters of God, called to give courageous witness to this in the way we live and love. We dare to hope that what Jesus did in his life will continue to be seen in the way we live our lives. We share the same spirit of God that moved in Jesus.

The church exists as a communion of people who believe these truths to be good news and worth spreading. The church community always tries to bring these insights and beliefs to our focus, and does so in many ways. We tell stories about God, about Jesus, and about the great men and women who have allowed the spirit of God to do marvelous deeds in their lives.

We have our rituals, our sacraments, and our liturgies. We have teaching, doctrine, and preaching. We have laws to preserve gospel values and to ensure good order. We have our religious customs and devotions. We have many forms of prayer. We have leadership and authority which try to "authorize" us into the truth of who we are as Christians. Our hope and expectation is that these features of church experience will lead people to focus on the three foundational Christian truths. The diagram illustrates the connection: B should always lead back to A.

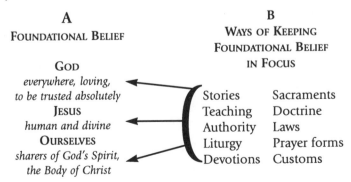

A	**B**
FOUNDATIONAL BELIEF	WAYS OF KEEPING
	FOUNDATIONAL BELIEF
GOD	IN FOCUS

A: FOUNDATIONAL BELIEF	B: Stories/etc.	B: Sacraments/etc.
GOD — *everywhere, loving, to be trusted absolutely*	Stories	Sacraments
JESUS — *human and divine*	Teaching	Doctrine
OURSELVES — *sharers of God's Spirit, the Body of Christ*	Authority	Laws
	Liturgy	Prayer forms
	Devotions	Customs

The three foundational beliefs (A) thus become for us the criteria by which we judge and evaluate the means we use to focus our attention on them (B). If we find our experience of B distracting us from A, or dividing and disappointing us, we need to question that experience. If we find ourselves being told or telling stories about God that make us fearful of God or lead us to imagine God being distant from us, we need to question the worth of those stories. If our religious customs and devotions suggest we have to buy God's mercy or win God's love, we need to ask why we have moved into this way of thinking and acting. If teaching and doctrine and preaching suggest that Jesus is not really as human as the rest of us are, we need to be alert to a shift from a foundational belief about Jesus.

If our participation in the liturgical and sacramental life of the church ever suggests we do not hold the treasure of God's presence, something radical has changed. If what we believe about real presence in the consecrated bread and speculation on how that happens ever becomes more important than our belief that we are the real presence of the Spirit of God in the world, let us acknowledge we have shifted focus from a foundational truth about ourselves. And if authority, leadership, and law are not experienced as supportive and life-giving as well as challenging, let us own the fact there has been a shift from their original purpose for existing.

The call to constantly evaluate our experience of Catholic belief and practice in light of the foundational truths challenges us both on a personal and communal level. Many of us would recognize that a significant part of our religious thinking was shaped by ideas, teaching, customs, images, and influences that distracted from the original focus of Christianity. The years since the Second Vatican Council have seen us discard some of that religious thinking, and church leadership at many levels has prompted us to do so. For some Catholics, however, this has been a painful time, especially for those whose Catholic identity relied heavily on the practices of the faith, rather than within the beliefs themselves. For them this time of dramatic change has not seemed like a spiritual renewal but rather like a dissipation of belief and practice. Gone is the clear emphasis on transubstantiation, purgatory, indulgences, grace, confession, benediction, rosary, mortal sin, Sunday obligation, clear sexual morality, and unquestioning loyalty to the pope.

There seems little doubt that future generations will look back to Vatican II and see it as a major turning point for the Catholic Church. Its effect was to thrust Catholics into a new way of being church. It initiated extraordinary changes in thinking and practice. In retrospect the church in general might have benefited more from the Council and prevented massive confusion and division if the faithful had been better prepared beforehand. Unfortunately, some of the leading scholars suggesting change in the decades prior to the Council were silenced by church authority on the grounds that their scholarship was dangerous to the faith of the "faithful."

Another important factor seems to have been that changes were initiated and explained after Vatican II, but the spirituality underlying the changes was not thoroughly preached, promoted, and accepted widely. In other words, the B column was modified with a change of practice or belief, but Catholics were not adequately led to focus on the A foundational beliefs on which change rested. Take, for example, the reintroduction of the Communion formula: the eucharistic minister says, "the Body of Christ," to which we reply, "Amen." Ask Catholics what they are saying "Amen" to, and the vast majority respond they are saying "yes" to the real presence of Jesus in the consecrated bread. They are surprised by the words of St. Augustine:

If you want to understand the body of Christ,
    listen to the apostle telling the faithful,
"You, though, are the body of Christ and its members."
So if it's you that are the body of Christ and its members,
    it's the mystery meaning *you* that has been placed
    on the Lord's table;
What you receive is the mystery that means you.
It is *to what you are* that you reply "Amen"
    and by so replying you express your assent.

What you hear is "the Body of Christ"
and you answer, "Amen."
So be a member of the body of Christ in order to make that
"Amen" true.[1] (emphasis added)

Here is a challenge to live a genuine Christian spirituality. It is the spirituality to which Vatican II called Catholics to immerse themselves, a spirituality that would bring renewal to the church. To the extent that Vatican II, alongside its great achievements in renewal of Catholic life, has also led to division, disappointment, and distraction in the Catholic Church today, this may well be because Catholics have not generally embraced that spirituality in sufficient depth.

Why is this so? Why is it that so many Catholics seem willing to stay at the level of B rather than embracing all of A wholeheartedly? The way we answer those questions will shape and clarify for us what we look for in church leadership in a new millennium.

LITERALISM IN THE CHURCH

A starting point in the search for answers is the issue of literalism in our religious images, and ways literalism has shaped our faith as a system of beliefs, our religious language, and our religious practice and devotions. We saw this literalism in the early chapters examining our images of God and in the chapters on Jesus. We seem to have lost the capacity to understand the role of and deal comfortably with myth, symbol, story, imagination, and mystery. For example, we took a classic myth about the creation of the world and we literalized it. Not only did we literalize it, we then built a whole theological system (as in B) around the literal interpretation.

The story of creation, as a myth, is marvelous, and we will always respect the way it puts us in touch with deep human realities such as sin, struggle, death, meaning, and relationship with a God who can at times seem to be loving, sometimes vengeful, sometimes demanding, sometimes close, sometimes distant. As myth it also has the capacity to relate us with other religious movements and their efforts to understand the transcendent. But literalize the story and not only do we appear foolish in the light of modern scientific evidence, but the whole theological and religious system of belief that depends on this literal understanding then comes into question. This in turn impinges on our understanding of Jesus as the God-figure who has to come down in order to change God's attitudes toward us.

Our literalism is evident also in the way we have imaged God as a localized being in the sky who speaks ("explicitly," says the *Catechism*) to a particular group of people or to specially chosen individuals. It is evident in our "he" language about God.

Literalism is again evident with our understanding of Jesus. Jesus of Nazareth opened people's minds and hearts to a unique sense of the transcendent. People of his time used story and symbol and myth to express their belief that Jesus shared in the fullness of God's life, that we, too, share in this, and that in death we will "know" this reality in a way we cannot now comprehend.

Story, symbol, and myth are used to open us to the larger dimension of mystery, wonder, imagination, and meaning. There are some stories in the Gospels which were never meant to be taken literally, for example, the story of Jesus walking on water, which became a proof story that Jesus was God, utterly different from the rest of us. The early Christians would have "heard" the story differently. They would have been far more attuned to the symbols of sea, storm, a small boat, and the realities of oppressive forces trying to overpower a small struggling community. Who or what is represented by the boat? Who or what does the wind symbolize? Who do we keep our eyes on in times of trouble? Who is Jesus for us? Stories like this give hope and encouragement to us as well as conveying who Jesus is and how he gives purpose to our lives. Their real power lies in the ability of the listener to think symbolically and to derive meaning that gives direction to life.

We have literalized the infancy accounts and the stories of Jesus' resurrection to such an extent that Catholics have enormous difficulty entering into the deepest meaning of these stories, e.g., where do we look to find the sacred? What is the nature of the sacred? "Story" here is not on the same level as Cinderella or Alice in Wonderland. People do not put their lives on the line for the story of Cinderella. Nor does story at that level have the capacity (or intention) to shape direction and meaning to life. Stories about the birth and resurrection of Jesus do precisely this. They were and are intended to evoke an adult faith response from people.

The power of the stories is lost when people ask questions such as, "Did it happen exactly like this?" This level of engagement, so common among Catholics, leads to pain, confusion, and disillusionment when people hear contemporary scholarship questioning the literal understanding of a particular story. Catholics cannot be blamed for their reaction. This is the way their church experience has led them to understand these stories.

Literalism is evident in the way our tradition has dealt with the existence of evil, sin, death, judgment, heaven, and hell. "Do you believe in the devil?" "Do you believe in a place called purgatory?" "Isn't there going to be a final judgment day when each of us will stand before God, and God will send the damned into hell?" These are all examples of the way our tradition has taken images dealing with the great mysteries of life and death and eternal life and literalized them. The functions listed in the B column have been influenced greatly by this literalism, and have thus shaped the religious worldview of many Christians. Questioning the literal truth or the literal understanding of the images then begins to undermine what for some people have always been very significant aspects of their religious worldview. They find it extremely difficult to shift from this level of faith to a deeper spirituality, even when this spirituality at the heart of our religion offers freedom and good news.

Popular thinking has carried this literalism into an understanding of the sacraments. "Sacraments are signs and symbols..." was the first part of the definition most of us learned about the sacraments. Despite this definition, literalism, especially concerning Eucharist, is very evident. It is not uncommon at the end of an adult education session on the

Eucharist to have someone ask, "Father, do you believe that after the consecration it is actually the real flesh and blood of Jesus on the altar?" Although there is a clear distinction between sacramental presence and actual physical presence in Catholic sacramental theology, it is not commonly understood. Some priests, and even the occasional bishop, are not too clear about the distinction. When the distinction is not understood people lapse into negative "*only* a symbol" comments which are dismissive of the ability of symbol to engage us with the mystery, reality, and presence of the transcendent. It becomes difficult, then, to convince people of what St. Augustine wrote: that it is "your mystery which has been placed on the altar." Instead we are led into disputes on *how* the presence of Jesus is in the bread. This becomes the issue, and we fail to recognize we have shifted our focus from the A to B.

The magnitude of the task facing leadership with regard to literalism cannot be overstated. There exists a huge gap in our church between the levels of popular faith and church scholarship. We can choose to keep scholarship away from "the simple faithful," or decide that a priority of leadership in a new millennium is to engage the faithful by challenging images and language that are barriers to a deeper spirituality. Isn't this what Jesus did?

Most of us would acknowledge two areas in particular that are important in this engagement. The first is being helped to know Jesus and Scripture better. The second, as we reexamine our religious images, ideas, and language, is being helped to appreciate how historical events, personalities, attitudes, and thought patterns shaped the way our faith has been packaged into a system of beliefs. Joseph Cardinal Ratzinger wrote in 1966 that one of the theological highlights of Vatican II was that: "Liturgical forms and customs, dogmatic formulations thought to have arisen with the apostles now appeared as products of complicated processes of growth within the womb of history."[2]

There is still much work to be done helping Catholics appreciate this particular highlight of the Council. It will surprise many

Catholics, for example, to hear that the doctrine of the Trinity was unknown to the apostles. It will also help us know why we believe what we believe, why we image the way we image, and how faithful our thinking and imaging are to the foundational truths of Christianity.

CHURCH AUTHORITY

The consideration to this point has been on personal faith. It is, however, in regard to the way the Catholic Church as an official, institutionalized religion sees itself in relationship with God, with other religions, and in the exercise of its official authority that the issue of literalism will also provide enormous challenges.

Catholic Church authority no longer enjoys center stage as it did in the Middle Ages, with enormous influence and control over western society. It is no longer given unquestioning obedience whenever it makes absolutist statements about moral behavior. And as Catholics today are being asked to take on more responsibility in the church, they want also a greater share in the decisions which affect their lives, their ministry, and the future of their parishes. This is a new phenomenon in the church, and there are clear signs indicating frustration and even resentment among many committed Catholics about the manner in which they encounter authority in their church today. We only have to compare the sense of promise and hope and pride in being Catholic at the end of the Second Vatican Council with the rise in anti-Rome sentiment prominent today to realize something has drastically changed.

The most fundamental issue is the status of Catholic Church authority at the top levels. This authority has rested on the claim of Catholicism being, in an exclusive way, the authoritative presence and voice of God working in the world. The Catholic Church now finds itself in a new position—of having to justify its claim to supreme religious authority. Previously, it had been enough to claim it, quoting texts of Scripture to "prove" it, supported by a religious worldview in which it made sense. Now it finds its claim being questioned, and the questioners are within as well as outside the church. Throughout the centuries, the Catholic tradition, in its teaching authority, has used its literal understanding of God as a Trinity of persons to show how the "Father" wants everyone to be Catholic because this is his "Son's Church." This is still part of the church's thinking as found in the *Catechism*:

> To reunite all his children, scattered and led astray by sin, the Father willed to call the whole of humanity together into his Son's Church. The Church is the place where humanity must rediscover its unity and salvation. The Church is "the world reconciled" (#845).

According to this line of thinking, the Catholic Church still sees itself as the only true and valid religion in the world. It recognizes the "search among shadows and images" for God in other religions, but considers that the goodness and truth found in other religions are "a preparation for the Gospel and given by him who enlightens all men that they may at length have life" (#843).

The Catholic Church's understanding of itself rests on the traditional belief that God the Father sent the Son down from heaven to save us. The Son of God founded the church. This church must therefore be the only true church, for no other church or religion in the world was founded by God himself.

We who are Catholic were educated to believe that the Catholic Church was the only genuine religion, and to be a member of this church was necessary for salvation, which we understood as entrance into heaven. Church authority was not to be questioned because church authority spoke in the name of God and therefore could not make mistakes when it commanded assent from Catholics. Our Catholic religious worldview led us to believe that the Spirit of God was nearer to and working more in church leaders than it was near to and working in the faithful. This understanding also allowed the Catholic Church to demand, as it has done consistently, total and unquestioning obedience.

We do not need a crystal ball to foresee enormous resistance within parts of the Catholic Church to scholarship which is now questioning the religious worldview which emphasizes Jesus as the Second Person of the Blessed Trinity. What is at stake is not merely doctrinal statements based on a literal understanding of the incarnation and the Blessed Trinity but the nature and place of Christianity and the Catholic Church in the world.

John Hick writes of the "great and...inescapable challenge" facing Christianity today:

(This) comes from new knowledge of the human religious world and of our continuity with that. This raises questions about the theological core of the Christianity that emerged out of the ecclesiastical debates and council decisions of the first five centuries: namely, that Jesus of Nazareth was God the Son living a human life. For from this there follows the world-centrality of Christianity as the only religion founded by God in person. It is here that the strain is now being felt. For Christianity's implicit or explicit claim to an unique superiority, as the central focus of God's saving activity on earth, has come to seem increasingly implausible within the new global consciousness of our time.[3]

It was mentioned in the first chapter that if we change our image of God in significant ways we are on dangerous ground. When that change of image touches on the Catholic Church's self-understanding as "the central focus of God's saving activity on earth," we have indeed moved on to dangerous ground. This understanding of itself has given church authority an enormous sense of power and control over people's lives. This power and control have come to be centralized in a very tight governing system that operates from above. One of the features of this style of authority has been intolerance of diversity.

Throughout its history the church has struggled with diversity. It has put enormous effort into controlling the way its members think and act. This conformity and uniformity became even more entrenched in the Catholic Church after the Reformation when church authority sought to keep control of its members.

Unquestioning loyalty, learning the catechism and knowing the answers, blind obedience to church authority, rigid observance of church laws, total adherence to strict liturgical laws, fear and guilt, and the use of Latin throughout the world all served to ensure an extraordinary state of conformity.

As an organization, the Catholic Church was a good example of the "functional" model. Preserving the good working of the institution was generally more important than any individual within the institution. Voices that disturbed or questioned the system of governance were not to be heard. There were clear cut divisions of power, and people knew who had the power. There was an emphasis on results and clear thinking. An idealized concept of what the church was deepened resistance to change. Why change what was divinely inspired and was operating smoothly?

Today we are experiencing a serious breakdown of a church culture built around conformity, uniformity, blind obedience to authority, religious attitudes that border on superstition, notions that the sacred is separate from human experience, and strict control over people's thinking and acting. There is a parallel here with what happened in the Middle Ages when people came to realize (through church influence, because the church stood to benefit) that kings were not divine rulers, but were laypeople like themselves. This marked the huge shift in society from the control of kings to church control. The historian R. W. Southern comments:

> It often happens at critical moments in history that ideas which have long held the field almost unchallenged are suddenly discovered, not to be wrong, but to be useless; then almost everyone can see they are absurd. So it was around the year 1100 AD. Even men with very little ability suddenly knew that the religious pretensions of kings had no foundation....
>
> It is amazingly simple to knock over cherished theories when they no longer satisfy the needs of the time. The thoughts on which royal government had acted for several centuries were blown away like airy nonsense. Almost no one bothered to

defend them. The old sacred kingship had no place in the new world of business.[4]

A mood akin to this is evident in the church today, and it is spreading. The mood is particularly evident among those in the thirty-to-fifty-year-old bracket. It is evident in their refusal to be tied to a Sunday Mass obligation under the pain of serious sin; in their refusal to allow church authority to discount their experience and sincerity; in their refusal to tolerate liturgies which do not nurture their faith or affirm God's presence with them; and in their refusal to work any longer with a system of governance which is not able to break new ground because it is locked into a theological worldview steadfastly resistant to change, e.g., on issues concerning priesthood.

Educators in adult faith development meet these people day after day and night after night at in-service programs for school principals, religious education coordinators and teachers, and in adult faith programs for parishioners. They are people seeking a more meaningful and cohesive understanding of their Catholic faith. They would gladly continue to be at the forefront of the church's life and ministry, but carry a mood of disappointment and discontent, and speak about a church system that is becoming more irrelevant to their lives.

The issue of youth participation in the church is often raised as *the* concern for the church today. Important as that is, it is becoming clear that the disenchantment of middle-age Catholics with the church is an even greater concern, needing urgent attention.

Much of this disenchantment has to do with the style of leadership and the way authority is exercised in the church today. Catholics are being asked to accept greater responsibility for the shape of "tomorrow's church." But they are finding again and again this is responsibility without a share in the power and the decision-making process. They can, for example, engage in discussions about whether parishes should merge, but find they are being asked to formulate solutions within narrow frames of reference, beyond which they are not allowed to think. The real power of decision making, the authority which decides, for example, that a community's right to Eucharist is less important than the Catholic Church requirement for celibate male priesthood, is beyond their influence.

A Mandate for Change

Here we are today, then, in the midst of enormous change, with a shift in worldview, images, and language that is unprecedented for centuries, in an age that is ready to question any authoritative statement. In many ways this time in the church parallels the Exodus experience: we have been called to leave the security of the immediate past (much of it contained in the B column) and journey into a time of wandering—a desert experience in many ways—looking for the Promised Land, shaping the church of the future.

We do not know when we will arrive; we do not know what shape will eventuate. What we focus on in the journey will either distract, divide, disappoint, and disillusion us or it will keep us together, hopeful, faithful, and committed. We know tomorrow's church cannot rest on outdated theology, yet it seems, at least to some committed Catholics, that their church has led them into a deeper spirituality only to keep blocking its effective public church witness by theological positions more connected with B than A.

Participation in decision making, being heard on important issues, allowing God's Spirit to be creative among us, and taking seriously that God's Spirit is active in the body of the church are all part of this deeper spirituality. This is what we see operating in the church at Pentecost.

Today in western society there is generally a shift to a growth model of organization. This model fits well with the spirituality of Pentecost. It has emphasis on the worth of the individual, giftedness, creating community, respecting differences while searching for what people have in common, creativity, and service of others. There is recognition that people will not accept being treated as objects by the institution. Appealing to personal responsibility, offering challenges to personal growth, and helping the individual to appreciate his or her talents—and then use them for the benefit of the institution and at the service of others—are important aspects of this model. Underlying all this is the fact that an organization or institution will function better in the long run if its members are nurtured, encouraged, and supported to recognize and utilize their potential, and if they are able to have a voice in the process of decision making on issues concerning them.

In August 1996, Joseph Cardinal Bernardin of Chicago called for a national conference in the United States to address issues which he said threatened the future of the Catholic Church. His expressed concern was the way church leadership is alienating the faithful by excluding debate on issues such as married clergy, ordination of women, church governance, organization of the liturgy, contraception and other questions dealing with sexuality, and dwindling church attendance. At a news conference, Bernardin stated:

> I have been troubled that an increasing polarization within the church and, at times, a mean spiritedness have hindered the kind of dialogue that helps us address our mission and concern.
>
> As a result, the unity of the church is threatened, the great gift of the Second Vatican Council is in danger of being seriously undermined, the faithful members of the church are weary and our witness to government, society and culture is compromised.[5]

Bernardin proposed that a document produced by the National Pastoral Life Center, entitled "Called to Be Catholic," be used as a framework to foster reflection on issues of concern.[6]

Cardinal Bernard Law of Boston said it was "unfortunate" that Bernardin's call had been linked with the "Called to Be Catholic" statement. Why? Because this statement "appeals for 'dialogue' as a path to 'common ground.'" Law stated,

> The church already has "common ground." It is found in the Sacred Scripture and Tradition, and is mediated to us through the authoritative and binding teaching of the Magisterium [the teaching authority of the church]....
>
> Dissent from revealed truth or the authoritative teaching of

the church cannot be "dialogued" away. Truth and dissent from truth are not equal partners in ecclesial dialogue. Dialogue as a way to mediate between the truth and dissent is mutual deception.[7]

Cardinal Law was joined by others in the hierarchy opposing Bernardin's initiative. When Bernardin died in November, the London *Tablet's* editorial commented on this opposition: "Can it be that the Catholic authorities have moved so far to the right that they suspect any call to the extreme center from which spring the deepest developments in the Church?"[8]

The deepest developments in the church today are not coming from what Cardinal Law restricts as "the common ground"—the package of doctrines and "authoritative teaching." The developments are coming from scholarship and research which has pertinent and insightful questions about the ways "common ground," as Cardinal Law understands it, has been packaged and on issues to which that "common ground" never had to attend in the past. There is not much point in church authority appealing to its "common ground" as if it were a fixed reality, a package of doctrinal belief it can hand on to generation after generation while ignoring contemporary questions and insights.

How do we talk about God in a society that has lost its sense of the sacred, and considers the religious worldview in which we have shaped our images and language about God to be nonsense? How do we talk about Jesus in a society that sees no need for a God-figure to come down from heaven to save us—especially when the salvation is connected with a God who supposedly locked us out of heaven? Is the sacred, divinity, God's presence, a reality that permeates all life, or does it primarily exist somewhere removed from us? Is God *actually* a Trinity of Persons, or is this a model to help us understand the mystery of God within specifically Christian experience?

What do we mean by "God"? What are we imaging? Does the Catholic Church have more of God's presence or approval than any other religion? On what grounds do we give our answer? Where should we look to experience the movement or presence of God? What does it mean to say that a human person, Jesus, is divine? What does divinity mean? Do we share in it? How do we take seriously the radical equality of women in the church today? Are there other specific contemporary questions which neither Scripture nor the Church's Tradition ever had to engage and debate?

These, and many others, are questions about "truth" today. They are "common ground" questions that connect us as members of the Catholic Church. They will connect us more if we are encouraged to engage the questions, search together, and try to find answers as responsible, committed Catholics. We might discover that "truth" is not a neatly parceled commodity for which one section of the church has the responsibility of sharing with the rest of us. We might discover that we are called to live with more questions, mystery, unknowns, and seeming contradictions than we ever imagined, but all of us will know we are committed to living the "truth" as we honestly engage it, and we will be grateful for people who help us in our search. We might even discover, as Michael Dowd believes, that

> The Christian movement today is still in the elementary stages of working out for itself and for the world the implications of the Gospel. There isn't the slightest doubt that the greatest and boldest creedal assertions are in the future, not the past.[9]

The pity is that such a statement would not find approval, or even be considered seriously, within sections of the upper reaches of the Catholic Church hierarchy today. God's surprises are finished. We have fully worked out and put into neat theological categories all there is ever to know about God. All future questions and issues can be dealt with within those categories.

We see this thinking at work in the "restorationist" approach in some sections of the church today. This is a "return to the past" movement, a yearning to recapture the splendor and the certainty which the church enjoyed before "modernism" and the age of questioning, disobedience, and individualism.

Restorationist voices in the Catholic Church (and elsewhere) rightly criticize the modern age for its excesses, especially its emphasis on personal freedom and its faith in reason and scientific technology to handle all problems. They rightly point out that the modern age cut itself off from the need and value of community which kept alive and promoted the wisdom of a particular tradition. Respect for the good order (hierarchy) which bound community together lessened, as did dependence on external authority. The restorationist response favors a strong, authoritative teaching method. The lament is that people— the young especially—do not know the faith; they do not know doctrine. We must teach it firmly and clearly. Knowledge of the tradition is very important.

This is a healthy conservatism voicing a genuine concern and need. If we cannot educate both children and adults into the basics of our Christian/Catholic tradition we can hardly call ourselves Christian/Catholic educators. And we must always be prepared to show that our teaching stands within that tradition.

Translating that need and concern into practice, though, is a different matter. The days of rote learning are gone. Many of the images and much of the language of religious faith make no sense to many teenagers and adults. We live in an age in which everything is questioned, and the days are certainly gone in which a religious educator could simply demand acceptance of the matter he or she presents. In fact, the teacher is sometimes not too sure what he or she believes on a particular topic. This is not only inevitable in a time of questioning, it is inevitable also when an authoritative resource such as the *Catechism* presents a worldview at odds with contemporary thinking.

As well as the call to return to clear, strong teaching accompanied by unquestioning acceptance, the restorationist approach to the problems in the church today calls also for a return to those highly visible, distinctive "Catholic" practices which in the past shaped identity for us: the rosary, Benediction, Holy Hour, clerical and religious dress, return to confessional practice, strong discipline, learning the catechism, processions, and distinctive forms of Marian devotion. The reasoning seems to be that these worked well in the past; all the troubles began in the church when we dropped them; let us return to them, and we will get on top of the problems. Vocations will increase, and we can get back into the style of church life we had before Vatican II turned everything upside down.

But there is no going back. Tomorrow's Catholics confront the enormous task of shaping their faith with respect for contemporary science, appreciation of myth, imagination, mystery, wonder, symbol and the power of story, the teaching of Jesus, a knowledge of the way faith came to be formulated into doctrines, and a deepened awareness of the Spirit of God in them. They will need help to sift the basics of Christian insight into the transcendent from literal interpretation and historical packaging. Actively promoting and providing this help, at all levels of Catholic life, may well be the biggest task the Catholic church faces in the new millennium.

The help *is* at hand, and it is at hand in mainstream Catholic theology.

Path for the Future

Mainstream Catholic theology has profound respect for the church's tradition, but it also shows a readiness to be radical, i.e., a willingness to investigate the roots (radical comes from the Latin word *radix*, meaning "root") that gave birth to a traditional belief or practice, and to examine what implications there might be in this. The lesson is that there may well be truly radical insights of value to the church today, gained by stirring through the embers of the "complicated processes" referred to by Cardinal Ratzinger. What may seem radical in the extreme for many people need not mean having no part in the church's tradition.

The mainstream stance is far more likely to be radical, in this sense, in the way it approaches Scripture and early church belief and practice. Whereas the restorationist might assert, "This is the way this (issue) has been, is, and always should be," contemporary scholarship is more likely to assert, "But these are the factors which gave birth to this belief or practice; these factors are no longer relevant to us today, so we do not have to be bound by that conclusion." Or, the approach might be: granted God's activity in human affairs is mysterious, beyond our imagination, constantly creative, never to be tied down into the confines of our human comprehension, there could be a turn we took and a road we followed in our history that led us to miss something, or to discount as unimportant what in fact was an important aspect of God's activity. Or, the Scripture scholar might say, "Granted what we know today about the way this text or story found its way into Scripture, we can no longer use it to defend a particular position or belief as we have done for a long time."

A consequence of this approach, though, is that it seems to the Catholic in the pews on Sunday that everything is being questioned. There is uncertainty about what to believe. What seemed to be rock-solid, unchangeable aspects of belief are now questioned or even discarded. One priest says one thing, and another priest teaches something else. Worse for some, the pope says one thing, and a priest says something else. It is not uncommon to hear: "Well, considering what you have just said, why should I believe anything I was taught anymore?" Sometimes this is by way of accusation that what has been heard cannot possibly be right. Sometimes it is expressing acceptance, but acknowledging the confusion the hearer now experiences.

History shows that one particular response to this confusion will not help the Catholic Church. That is the response which says: let us silence all the voices which cause confusion in people and let us insist that the "common ground"—understood as a package of truths—be taught and learned. The teaching authority of the Catholic Church can hardly expect to prepare future generations to embrace its faith if it silences voices raising questions that are grounded in the roots of the church's practice and tradition, as well as questions that emerge from a dramatically changed worldview and cultural shifts in attitudes.

Today's Catholics are suffering the ill effects of the silencing that has been very evident in our church this century. This silencing and unwillingness to promote new learning among the faithful has resulted in Catholics remaining abysmally ignorant of Scripture and its formation, ignorant about the way historical events shaped belief and practices, and almost totally unprepared for the massive changes that came with the Second Vatican Council. They consequently find themselves very limited in basic theological understanding on controversial issues of faith and morals.

Take, for example, questions concerning whether Jesus knew or thought he was God and how the doctrine of the Trinity became fixed in the Christian Creed. What is most likely to happen, at many levels of the Catholic Church today, is for discussion to be blocked. The very idea that questions could be raised will be labeled as heretical by some people, and people will be quoted out of context to show how heretical they are. Yet, underlying a topic such as this is the deeper issue: will Catholic leadership provide opportunities for adults to engage in discussion and will contemporary scholarship be brought to these discussions? Or will Catholics be kept in ignorance of theological voices that respectfully suggest there are other ways of considering beliefs, attitudes, and practices that had seemed set in concrete?

Consider the way Roman authority has "played God" on the issue of women's ordination. The impression is given that this authority really knows the mind of God, and even God's mind cannot be changed on this issue. Part of the reasoning for the ban on women being ordained is the fact that Jesus did not ordain women. This reasoning simply glosses over contemporary scholarship which suggests "it (is) very doubtful that (Jesus) intended to lay down such a particular prescription regarding the sex of future candidates for ordination or indeed that he explicitly set up the practice of ordination itself."[10]

Again, it is not just the topic that is important in its own right. It is the underlying issue: will church authority allow respected, dissenting, scholarship to be heard by the faithful? So far the answer, on this particular topic, is a definite negative. There exists a ban on public discussion of this issue, and a priest daring to break the ban may find his faculties to preach in a diocese being removed. Dissent is viewed as disloyalty.

Church authority, on all levels, would go a long way to winning the respect of adult Catholics if it exhibited a willingness to listen and learn, an openness to new insights and points of view, and tolerance of divergent thinking when there is evidence to support that thinking.

Scripture, Jesus, and the reality of God's loving presence in our world are foundations to our Christian faith. Shouldn't we expect, then, that all people who exercise authority and leadership in our church be open to scholarship in Scripture studies, and encourage Catholics to embrace the insights of those studies? Shouldn't we expect them to acknowledge the urgent need to present Jesus and his work of salvation in thought patterns that are not dependent on an outmoded worldview? Shouldn't they persistently and confidently proclaim the good news that the spirit of God moves in all people? Should not Catholics be challenged to witness to a strong moral code because they are first of all helped to develop a strong conviction of their own sacredness?

Many Catholics hope for such leadership at all levels in their church. Some want to give their time and talents in the service of leadership. They want to experience and participate in a church whose leadership and teaching authority is strong, relevant, supportive, and challenging.

In his bestseller, *Care of the Soul*, Thomas Moore writes of the importance of teachers being "mentor" to their students. His words touch the quality many people long to see in church authority and leadership:

> Some teachers don't seem to understand the need in their students to be on an odyssey and to be discovering their own fatherhood. They expect their students to be a copy of themselves and to profess the same values and information. Some business and political leaders see their role in society as promoting their own personal ideologies rather than serving as genuine mentors; they don't understand that the populace must make its own collective odyssey in order to evoke a soulful fatherhood for the society. It takes genuine wisdom to be a mentor, the pleasure of which comes from instilling fatherhood rather than embodying it.[11]

Jesus certainly did not expect Peter to be a copy of himself. We have in the relationship between them a perfect example of the mentoring style of leadership. Look what it produced in Peter. Jesus' style put a great deal of trust in human nature's ability to allow goodness and growth and wisdom to win through. Good authority trusts—even when some failure is inevitable. Jesus initially trusted Judas as well as Peter.

The realization of the hopes many Catholics have for the style of leadership and authority in the church rests on the promotion of a genuine spirituality throughout the church. Genuine in the sense that it have the heart and soul—and the risk-taking and trust—of Pentecost. This is what the church exists for. This is what the church is called to be good at. This spirituality, based on the foundational Christian beliefs about God, Jesus, and ourselves, ought to be the norm we return to when we evaluate our preaching, our liturgies, our collective ownership of being church, and our openness to change. Are we consistently giving witness in all these activities that the sacred is in our midst? Does leadership and authority consistently affirm and encourage the faithful with this truth? Does it trust the faithful with it? Do our liturgies reflect the joy of it? Is all our parochial ministry firmly founded on the belief that the sacred is found in everyone?

The "common ground" in a Christian context has to do with belief in God, the nature of our relationship with God, our relationship with Jesus, our belief in ourselves as sons and daughters of God, the meaning we give to life, and the role of the church. If these are the content of our search, then our ability to engage the truth will surely depend on our readiness to ask questions, to search more, to keep expanding our knowledge, to trust our own experiences of life, to learn from the wisdom of the religious tradition in which we stand, and to break from images, worldviews, and thought patterns that are no longer relevant to our times.

In a willingness to relinquish its claims to exclusivity, in an admission that it does not hold a monopoly on religious truth, in an openness to the reality of God's presence everywhere, and in the belief that God's presence is constantly creative and beyond our present imagining, the Catholic Church could be a renewed beacon of hope and leadership in our world. The Gospel image of being willing to die in order to bear new fruit might just be part of the challenge facing the Catholic Church in this millennium. It has, with the rest of Christianity, a message of salvation to offer. That message, and the spirituality of Pentecost, is good news for all the world. It could be offered to the world in the conviction that the Catholic Church stands compassionately with all of humankind and with all religions in the search for truth about the God we reverence in awesome wonder.

But if we are to stand compassionately with the rest of the world, part of our task will be to present our message in a worldview with which the rest of the world can resonate. Contemporary cosmology offers such a framework. So do the great stories about God and Jesus, the insights and wisdom contained in our Christian tradition, and our Catholic sacramental system—provided we free them from literalism and dualistic thought patterns.

All these combined could lead us *beyond* ourselves into awesome wonder as we engage the mystery of a God beyond all imagining, *into* ourselves as we contemplate the wonder of who we are, and *toward* *others* as we accept the challenge of incarnating God's presence on earth as courageously and lovingly as a man who died on a cross two thousand years ago.

NOTES

1. *The Works of Saint Augustine: A Translation for the 21st Century.* Sermons. III/7, translation and notes by Hill, Edmund O.P.; J. Rotelle O.S.A., ed. (New York: New City Press, 1993), p. 300.
2. Ratzinger, Joseph, *Highlights of Vatican II* (Mahwah, NJ: Paulist Press Deus Books, 1966), p. 99.
3. Hick, *The Metaphor of God Incarnate*, p. 7
4. Southern, R. W., "Western Society and the Church in the Middle Ages," *The Pelican History of the Church*, vol. 2 (Middlesex, England: Penguin Books, 1970), p. 37.
5. The *Boston Globe*, Tuesday, August 13, 1996, p. A8.
6. cf *Origins*, vol. 26, no. 11; August 29, 1996, p. 166f.
7. The *Pilot*, Friday, August 16, 1996, p. 16.

8. The *Tablet*, 23 November 1996, p. 1531.

9. Dowd, *Earthspirit*, p. 25.

10. Catholic Theological Society of America, "Tradition and Women's Ordination: A Question of Criteria," draft paper in *Origins*, vol. 26, no. 6, June 27, 1996, p. 92.

11. Moore, Thomas, *Care of the Soul: A Guide for Cultivating Depth and Sacredness in Everyday Life* (New York: HarperCollins, 1994), p. 38.

REFLECTION

1. In what ways have I shifted from literal images and thought patterns? Who or what helped me to shift? How is my new understanding helping me?

2. What literal images and thought patterns am I presently finding difficult to shift from? What is making me hold on to them?

3. In what ways does the (B) and (A) diagram help understanding of change in the church today?

4. What ideas in the book have enthused me? What ideas have disturbed me? Why? To what area of interest, study or need for further information has it now led me? How will I pursue this?

RECOMMENDED READING

1. Moore, Thomas; *Care of the Soul.*

2. Bokenkotter, Thomas; *A Concise History of the Catholic Church.*

3. Bokenkotter, Thomas; *Dynamic Catholicism.* (Former title was *Essential Catholicism.*)

4. Campbell, Joseph; *Myths To Live By.*

Bibliography

Andersen, Frank. *Jesus, Our Story.* Melbourne: Dove Books, 1994. (US edition: *Imagine Jesus.* Liguori Publications, Liguori, MO, 1996).

Arbuckle, Gerald. *Refounding the Church: Dissent for Leadership.* Maryknoll, NY: Orbis Books, 1993.

Armstrong, Karen. *A History of God.* New York: Ballantine Books, 1993.

Berry, Thomas. *The Dream of the Earth,* paperback ed.. San Francisco: Sierra Club Books, 1990.

Birch, Charles. *On Purpose.* Sydney: New South Wales University Press Ltd., 1990.

Bokenkotter, Thomas. *A Concise History of the Catholic Church,* rev. ed. New York: Doubleday, 1977.

Bokenkotter, Thomas. *Dynamic Catholicism.* New York: Doubleday, 1992. (Former title was *Essential Catholicism: Dynamics of Faith and Belief.*)

Boorstin, Daniel J. *The Discoverers: A History of Man's Search to Know His World and Himself.* New York: Vintage Books, 1985.

Brown, Raymond. *Biblical Exegesis & Church Doctrine.* Mahwah, NJ: Paulist Press, 1985.

Brown, Raymond. *Biblical Reflections on Crises Facing the Church.* Mahwah, NJ: Paulist Press, 1975.

Brown, Raymond. *The Critical Meaning of the Bible.* Mahwah, NJ: Paulist Press, 1991.

Brown, Raymond. *An Introduction to New Testament Christology.* Mahwah, NJ: Paulist Pres. 1994.

Brown, Raymond. *Responses to 101 Questions on the Bible.* Mahwah, NJ: Paulist Press, 1990.

Byrne, Brendan J. *Inheriting the Earth: The Pauline Basis of a Spirituality for Our Time.* Staten Island, NY: Alba House, 1990.

Campbell, Joseph. *Myths To Live By.* New York: Penguin Books, 1993.

Capra, Fritjof and David Steindl-Rast, with Thomas Matus. *Belonging to the Universe: Explorations on the Frontiers of Science and Spirituality.* San Francisco: HarperSanFrancisco, 1992.

Catechism of the Catholic Church. Collegeville, MN: The Liturgical Press, 1994.

Dawes, Hugh. *Freeing The Faith: A Credible Christianity For Today.* London: SPCK, 1992.

De Mesa, Jose. *Doing Theology: Basic Realities and Processes.* Quezon City, Philippines: Claretian Publications, 1990.

de Saint-Exupéry, Antoine. *Wind, Sand and Stars,* reprint ed. Cutchogue, NY: Buccaneer Books, 1992.

Donovan, Vincent J. *Christianity Rediscovered.* Maryknoll, NY: Orbis Books, 1982.

Donovan, Vincent J. *The Church in the Midst of Creation.* Maryknoll, NY: Orbis Books, 1989.

Dowd, Michael. *Earthspirit: A Handbook for Nurturing an Ecological Spirituality.* Mystic, CT: Twenty-Third Publications, 1991.

Dulles, Avery. *Models of Revelation,* second ed. Maryknoll, NY: Orbis Books, 1992.

Dunn, James D. *The Parting of the Ways Between Christianity and Judaism and their Significance for the Character of Christianity.* London: SCM Press, 1991.

Edwards, Denis. *Jesus and the Cosmos.* Mahwah, NJ: Paulist Press, 1992.

Edwards, Denis. *Jesus, the Wisdom of God: An Ecological Theology.* Maryknoll, NY: Orbis Books, 1995.

Edwards, Denis. *Made From Stardust: Exploring the Place of Human Beings Within Creation.* N. Blackburn, Australia: Collins Dove, 1992.

Feuerstein, Georg and Trisha Lamb Feuerstein. *Voices on the Threshold of Tomorrow: One Hundred Forty-Five Views of the New Millennium.* Wheaton, IL: Quest Books, 1993.

Fiorenza, Francis S. and John P. Galvin, eds. *Systematic Theology: Roman Catholic Perspectives,* 2 vols. Minneapolis, MN: Augsburg Fortress Press, 1991.

Fitzmyer, Joseph A. *Scripture and Christology: A Statement of the Biblical Commission with a Commentary*. Mahwah, NJ: Paulist Press, 1986.

Fowler, James. *Weaving the New Creation: Stages of Faith and the Public Church*. San Francisco: HarperSanFrancisco, 1991.

Fries, Heinrich. *Suffering From the Church: Renewal or Restoration?* Collegeville, MN: The Liturgical Press, 1995.

Goosen, Gideon and Margaret Tomlinson. *Studying the Gospels: An Introduction*. Ridgefield, CT: Morehouse Publications, 1994.

Greeley, Andrew M. *The Great Mysteries: An Essential Catechism*, rev. ed. San Francisco: HarperSanFrancisco, 1985.

Greeley, Andrew. *The Jesus Myth*. London: Search Press, 1972.

Gribbin, John. *In the Beginning: The Birth of the Living Universe*. London: Penguin Books, 1994.

Griffin, David, William Beardsley, and Joe Holland. *Varieties of Postmodern Theology*. Albany, NY: State University of New York Press, 1989.

Griffiths, Bede. *The Cosmic Revelation: The Hindu Way to God*. Springfield, IL: Templegate Publishers, 1983.

Griffiths, Bede. *A New Vision of Reality*. Springfield, IL: Templegate Publishers, 1990.

Guarino, Thomas G. *Revelation and Truth: Unity and Plurality in Contemporary Theology*. Scranton, PA: University of Scranton Press, 1993.

Hall, Thor. *The Evolution of Christology*. Nashville, TN: Abingdon Press, 1982.

Hegy, Pierre M., ed. *The Church in the Nineties: Its Legacy, Its Future*. Collegeville, MN: The Liturgical Press, 1993.

Hellwig, Monika. *Jesus, The Compassion of God: New Perspectives on the Tradition of Christianity*. Collegeville, MN: The Liturgical Press, 1983.

Hessel, Dieter, ed. *After Nature's Revolt: Eco-Justice and Theology*. Minneapolis, MN: Augsburg Fortress Press, 1992.

Hick, John. *The Metaphor of God Incarnate: Christology in a Pluralistic Age*. Louisville, KY: Westminster John Knox Press, 1993.

Hopkins, Julie. *Towards a Feminist Christology: Jesus of Nazareth, European Women, and the Christological Crisis*. Grand Rapids, MI: William B. Eerdmans Publishing Company, 1995.

Johnson, Elizabeth. *She Who Is: The Mystery of God in Feminist Theological Discourse*. New York: Crossroad Publications, 1994.

Johnson, Luke Timothy. *The Real Jesus Is the Christ of Faith*. San Francisco: HarperSanFrancisco, 1996.

Kasper, Walter. *The God of Jesus Christ*. New York: Crossroad Publications, 1992.

Kelly, Kevin T. "Archbishop Worlock's Legacy to Liverpool." *The Month*, April 1996.

Kelly, Tony. *An Expanding Theology: Faith in a World of Connections*. Ridgefield, CT: Morehouse Publishing, 1993.

Küng, Hans. *Credo: The Apostles' Creed Explained For Today*. London: SCM Press, 1993.

Küng, Hans. *Christianity: Essence, History and Future*. New York: Continuum Publications, 1996.

Lonergan, Anne and Caroline Edwards, eds. *Thomas Berry and the New Cosmology*. Mystic, CT: Twenty-Third Publications, 1987.

Lyon, David. *Postmodernity*. Minneapolis, MN: University of Minnesota Press, 1994.

Macquarrie, John. *Jesus Christ in Modern Thought*. London: SCM Press, 1990.

McBrien, Richard. *The Remaking of the Church*. New York: Harper and Row, 1973.

McFague, Sallie. *The Body of God: An Ecological Theology*. Minneapolis, MN: Augsburg Fortress Press, 1993.

Metz, Johann Baptist. *The Emergent Church*. New York: Crossroad Publications, 1986.

Moore, Thomas. *Care of the Soul: A Guide for Cultivating Depth and Sacredness in Everyday Life*. New York: HarperCollins, 1994.

Myers, Ched. *Binding the Strong Man: A Political Reading of Mark's Story of Jesus*. Maryknoll, NY: Orbis Books, 1988.

Neuner, J. and Dupuis J. *The Christian Faith: Doctrinal Documents of the Catholic Church*, 5th & enlarged ed. London: HarperCollins Religious, 1992.

Nolan, Albert. *Jesus Before Christianity*. Maryknoll, NY: Orbis Books, 1978.

O'Grady, John. *Models of Jesus Revisited*. Mahwah, NJ: Paulist Press, 1994.

O'Murchu, Diarmuid. *The God Who Becomes Redundant*. Dublin: The Mercier Press Ltd., 1986.

O'Murchu, Diarmuid. "A New Spirituality For Our Newly Emerging World." *The Teilhard Review*; Summer 1984, vol. 29, no. 2.

Ormerod, Neil. "The Transcultural Significance of the Definition of Chalcedon." *The Australasian Catholic Record*; July 1993.

Perkins, Pheme. *Gnosticism and the New Testament*. Minneapolis, MN: Augsburg Fortress Press, 1993.

Polkinghorne, John. *Science and Christian Belief: Theological Reflections of a Bottom-up Thinker*. London: SPCK, 1994. (US edition: *The Faith of a Physicist: Reflections of a Bottom-up Thinker*. Princeton, NJ: Princeton University Press, 1994.)

Pontifical Biblical Commission. *The Interpretation of the Bible in the Church*. Boston: St. Paul Books and Media, 1993. (cf. Fitzmyer, Joseph A. *Scripture and Christology*)

Portier, William. *Tradition and Incarnation: Foundations of Christian Theology*. Mahwah, NJ: Paulist Press, 1994.

Ratzinger, Joseph. *Highlights of Vatican II*. Mahwah, NJ: Paulist Press Deus Books, 1966.

Schreiter, Robert, ed. *The Schillebeeckx Reader*. New York: Crossroad Publications, 1984.

Segundo, Juan Luis. *The Historical Jesus of the Synoptics*. Maryknoll, NY: Orbis Books, 1985.

Snyder, Mary Hembrow. *The Christology of Rosemary Radford Ruether: A Critical Introduction*. Mystic, CT: Twenty-Third Publications, 1988.

Southern, R. W. "Western Society and the Church in the Middle Ages," *The Pelican History of the Church*, vol. 2. Middlesex, England: Penguin Books, 1970.

Swimme, Brian. *The Hidden Heart of the Cosmos: Humanity and the New Story*. Maryknoll, NY: Orbis Books, 1996.

Swimme, Brian. *The Universe Is a Green Dragon: A Cosmic Creation Story*. Santa Fe, NM: Bear & Company, 1984.

Swimme, Brian and Thomas Berry. *The Universe Story: From the Primordial Flaring Forth to the Ecozoic Era-A Celebration of the Unfolding of the Universe*. San Francisco: HarperSanFrancisco, 1994.

Thompson, William M. *The Jesus Debate: A Survey & Synthesis*. Mahwah, NJ: Paulist Press, 1985.

Tracy, David. ed. with Hans Küng and J. B. Metz. "Toward Vatican III," *Concilium*. New York: The Seabury Press, 1978.

Tracy, David and Nicholas Lash, eds. "Cosmology and Theology," *Concilium: Religion in the Eighties*. New York: The Seabury Press, 1983.

The Works of Saint Augustine: A Translation for the 21st Century. Sermons. III/7, translation and notes by Hill, Edmund O.P.; J. Rotelle O.S.A., ed. New York: New City Press, 1993.

Wright, David. "Councils and Creeds," in *The History of Christianity: A Lion Handbook*, Tim Dowley, ed. Tring, Herts, England: Lion Publishing, 1988.

Wright, N.T. *Who Was Jesus?* Grand Rapids, MI: William B. Eerdmans Publishing Company, 1993.

Index

Brave New Church
From Turmoil to Trust
William J. Bausch

Here popular author William J. Bausch charts a direction for the Catholic church to follow in years to come. He begins this work by focusing on fourteen challenges facing the Church today, including religious illiteracy, anti-Catholicism, secularism, pluralism, Church scandal, and authority. Bausch then considers the transitions and responses that can move the Church forward as it seeks to minister to the world of the twenty-first century. Written in a clear, informative, and uplifting style the book is peppered throughout with anecdotes, parables, and citations from news stories and reports.

320 pages, $16.95 (J-85)

Catholics in Crisis?
The Church Confronts Contemporary Challenges
William J. Bausch

Here Bausch addresses movements such as new age, fundamentalism, and "end-of-the-world mania." He examines both the negative and positive aspects of these issues, then goes on to show how a weakened Church has difficulty meeting the challenges that arise from them. In the last chapter Bausch makes practical suggestions on how to overcome these difficulties.

240 pages, $14.95 (order J-13)

The Parish of the Next Millennium
William J. Bausch

Summarizes the social and cultural forces shaping our lives and church by examining where we are and where we might be going. Catalogues the issues dealt with in church and society today, and gives concrete signs of hope and rebirth for the next millennium.

304 pages, $16.95 (order M-93)

A Radical Challenge for Priesthood Today
From Trial to Transformation
William D. Perri

A psychotherapist offers a challenging assessment of a revered Church institution. For priesthood to function as it must, Perri suggests that transformation is essential. He believes that a humble recognition and acceptance of current problems can become the source for a richer and more meaningful expression of priesthood.

144 pages, $14.95 (order B-16)